An Introduction to LITERARY CRITICISM

by

S. M. SCHREIBER

PERGAMON PRESS

OXFORD · LONDON · EDINBURGH · NEW YORK
TORONTO · PARIS · FRANKFURT

Pergamon Press Ltd., Headington Hill Hall, Oxford
4 & 5 Fitzroy Square, London W.1

Pergamon Press (Scotland) Ltd., 2 & 3 Teviot Place, Edinburgh 1
Pergamon Press Inc. 44-01 21st Street, Long Island City, New York 11101
Pergamon of Canada Ltd., 6 Adelaide Street East, Toronto, Ontario
Pergamon Press S.A.R.L., 24 rue des Ecoles, Paris 5e
Pergamon Press GmbH, Kaiserstrasse 75, Frankfurt-am-Main

First edition 1965
Reprinted with corrections February 1966
Library of Congress Catalog Card No. 65-22539

Printed in Great Britain by Billing and Sons Ltd., Guildford and London

(381/66)

To

ROSALIND CLAY

without whose encouragement
this book would not have been completed

CONTENTS

PREFACE

THIS book had its origin in a course of classes which I gave to groups of girls who were preparing for the Oxford and Cambridge Entrance Examination in Classics, Modern Languages and English. I found that although my pupils had a detailed knowledge of the various books set for the examinations, including sometimes the works of individual critics, the majority knew little or nothing of the general literary principles at the back of the particular judgements which they had, generally, taken on trust. They knew that *Hamlet* was "a great tragedy"; those doing French knew that Racine's tragedies were "great". But as to whether Shakespeare or Racine had anything in common which accounted for the "greatness", or even what (apart from death at the end) makes a play a tragedy, they were either completely ignorant or else repeated clichés of which they did not know the meaning. And from their response I had little doubt that the classes "fulfilled a need". Again and again I found that they were excited by the discovery that there were reasons at the back of the judgements which they had been given and answers to the questions which they had, possibly, done little more than vaguely formulate.

My intention when I set out to write this book was that it should be used in the sixth forms of schools. But in the course of several revisions it has quite outgrown its original purpose; I found that I was able to develop the various sections considerably more fully than was either possible or necessary in preparing immature girls for examinations, and in its present form I hope that it may be of use not only to schoolboys and schoolgirls but to the general reader. It still retains, however, some marks of its origin in its occasional pedagogical manner; if mature readers should feel that I am "writing down" to them I would ask them to remember how the book came into being.

No one can know better than I do that the book is full of oversimplifications. I think that this is inevitable in an elementary introduction. But whenever I have been aware of oversimplification or the appearance of dogmatism on controversial subjects, I have done my best to give fair warning that the matter is not so simple and cut-and-dried as I may have made it appear. My aim has been, not the impossible one of giving a complete and uncontroversial answer to every question which arises in the book, but to give pointers in what I believe to be the right direction and to stimulate interest and curiosity and the desire to explore further.

As English Literature is my own subject I have inevitably drawn the greater number of my illustrations, especially in the realm of critical writing, from English authors. But, besides drawing upon what knowledge I have of other literatures, I have tried as far as I was able so to state the general critical problems and principles that students studying a foreign language should be able to discover for themselves their application to the books they read.

S. M. S.

ACKNOWLEDGEMENTS

My thanks are due to the following for permission to use copyright material: to the Clarendon Press, Oxford, for extracts from Bywater's translation of Aristotle *On the Art of Poetry*; to Messrs. Rupert Hart-Davis Ltd. for passages from Humphry House's *Aristotle's Poetics*; to Messrs. Macmillan & Co. Ltd. and the Trustees of the Hardy Estate for *In the Time of "The Breaking of Nations"* from *The Collected Poems of Thomas Hardy*; to Mrs. Middleton Murry for a passage from *John Clare and Other Studies*; to Messrs. Jonathan Cape Ltd. for passages from Cecil Day Lewis's *The Poetic Image*; to Messrs. Edward Arnold Ltd. for a passage from E. M. Forster's *Aspects of the Novel*; to Messrs. Martin Secker & Warburg Ltd., and Messrs. Harcourt, Brace & World of New York for passages from Lascelles Abercrombie's *The Theory of Poetry*.

I regret that in the case of *On Some South African Novelists* by Roy Campbell I have been unable to trace the copyright holder. I tender my apologies for quoting it without permission and will rectify this in future editions should it be possible to do so.

CHAPTER I

WHAT IS LITERARY CRITICISM?

THIS book must begin with a preliminary warning: literary criticism is not something which can be summed up in a series of neat little statements which can be learnt by heart; rather, it is a journey of exploration into the nature of literature in all its variety; the last word is never said. What this book sets out to do is not to take you to the end of that journey and tell you what you will find there—it has no ending—but rather to set up a series of signposts so that you may start out in the right direction. I shall have to generalize, to over-simplify, sometimes to dogmatize: there will not be space to qualify every statement, or to give every side of controversial questions. But if you treat the book as what it is intended to be, not as a summary of the unsummarizable but as pointing the way to further reading and further thought, you will find out for yourselves the complexities and apparent contradictions, the paradoxical exceptions to the rule, which I have been obliged to ignore. You may even, in certain cases, decide after further reading that I have been mistaken. That will not matter: what matters is that you should be sufficiently stimulated to follow up the problems for yourselves. The book will only have failed if it does not make you want to go further along the various roads to which it points you.

This said, we go on to the subject of this chapter: What is Literary Criticism? Of what use is it? And, assuming that it has a use, what are the qualifications of a critic? And how does he set about his job?

The Functions of Literary Criticism

The business of the literary critic is, in the first instance, to distinguish between a good book and a bad one, and, that done, to help us to recognize for ourselves, and to get full value out of, literary quality when we meet with it, thus opening up for us the whole world of pleasure and imaginative experience and intellectual stimulus which is waiting to be explored but which, without a qualified critic's help, we would not discover for ourselves. The ways in which the critic sets about his task are innumerable, ranging from, on the one hand, the most general statement of principle to, on the other, a detailed line by line and word by word analysis of one short poem, but always the purpose is the same: to quicken and refine our, the readers', perceptiveness so that, as time goes on, we too may come to share his understanding of, and pleasure in, what is best in literature. As Cecil Day Lewis puts it (*The Poetic Image*, p. 16): "To say it quite simply, the critic has one pre-eminent task—the task of *easing or widening or deepening our response to poetry*" (italics mine)—or, one must add, to whatever other branch of literature he may have chosen as his special study.

The Critic as Judge: Absolute Standards in Literature

I said in the last paragraph that the critic must, in the first instance, be able to distinguish between a good book and a bad one. The word "critic" is, in fact, derived from the Greek *critês*, a judge. Self-evidently the first step towards "easing or widening or deepening" our response to what is best in literature must be that the critic himself should be able to recognize quality when he meets with it. The first step only—but if he himself has not learnt to recognize the good and to reject what is worthless he will be a blind leader of the blind.

How, then, does a critic set about his task of judging? By what standards does he judge? And how are we, his readers, to know whether any given critic's judgement is likely to be more reliable than that of another or than our own?

These questions raise the whole problem of the existence of *absolute standards in literature*. And there are people who doubt whether such standards exist: they believe that the most that any critic can do is to express a personal preference for one book rather than for another, but that of whether one book is *in itself* better than another there is no method of proof. And this because of the subjective nature of the evidence upon which the critic must base his judgement. When a judge gives a verdict in a court of law the process is objective: he is guided, not by something personal to himself, but by a set of external laws* set down in black and white and familiar to every lawyer, and by sworn *statements of fact*; his own personal opinion only comes into play in assessing the reliability of any witness, and this can be checked by the evidence of other witnesses. The law forbids murder; all that concerns the judge is to discover whether the man in the dock did, in fact, commit murder or not; his own personal feelings about murder, or his liking for, or dislike of, the accused, are totally irrelevant. The critic, on the other hand, has no law to administer; the nearest thing to law which he has to guide him is certain statements of principle, such as those found in Aristotle's *Poetics*, but every critic who has treated these as the judge treats the law of the land, as external rules by which the (aesthetic) guilt or innocence of a writer can be determined, has invariably given mistaken judgements.† And the only evidence upon which a critic can base his judgement lies in his own personal response to what he reads: he asks, not "What are the rules? Does this work observe them?", but "What do I, the critic, feel about this book?" He may, it is true, if other critics whose opinion he respects differ from him, reserve judgement, but nevertheless the ultimate test is subjective. And this inevitably, for literature, whether poetry or prose, is addressed to the imaginative and

* Precedent apart, and that too is objective, something external to the judge.

† This point will be expanded in the later section, *The Critic as Generalizer.*

aesthetic sense of the individual reader and only the reader himself can judge of its impact.

Here lies the problem: if the test by which the critic judges is purely subjective—a matter not of externally verifiable facts but solely of his own personal preference—who is to say, should two critics disagree, or, as frequently happens, should the consensus of critical opinion differ from that of the general public, that any given critic's personal response is likely to be more reliable than that of another or of the non-critical majority? Is there, in fact, any objective standard by which we can say that some books are, in themselves, good and others bad, or is it, as many people claim, "all a matter of taste"? If there is no objective test of quality, and enjoyment is all, is there any evidence that *Hamlet* is a better play than *The Mousetrap* or *War and Peace* a better novel than Daphne du Maurier's *Rebecca*? Is not the critic's preference—and ours—for *Hamlet* and *War and Peace* simply a personal idiosyncrasy? Why should he—and we—be right and the majority—for they are a vast majority—who prefer *The Mousetrap* and *Rebecca* be wrong? If we can find no answer to these questions then value-judgement becomes a chimera—all that is possible is a statement of personal preferences, one as valid as another: a book is a good book for those who like it, a bad one for those who do not—in fact, "Every man his own critic".

But there is an answer to these questions. To find it we must break the vicious circle of subjectivity. And the circle can be broken if we can find, despite the subjectivity of the individual judgement, that there is objective evidence that, irrespective of what you or I or the man in the street may feel about them, some books *have proved themselves* to be better than others. If such evidence exists and we can identify these books, then the man or woman who prefers them to the rest has shown that he or she can recognize quality when they meet with it; those who do not, cannot—their judgement is worthless.

And such evidence does exist: the test of time. In every period there are books—the vast majority—which are enormously popular and which, at the time, produce a strong emotional response in the majority of their readers, but which, after a generation or two, are either completely forgotten or, if they survive at all, do so only as literary curiosities, evidence of the queer taste of our forbears.They have pleased only the contemporaries for whom they were written. But meantime other books throughout the centuries or even millennia have continued to be as moving and satisfying as they were to the people to whom they were first addressed. Such are the works of Homer, Aeschylus, Sophocles, Euripides, Virgil, Dante, Shakespeare, Racine, Milton—you can add to the list. Their readers have belonged to different races, and in some cases to periods of history far remote from those which gave them birth, living in totally different circumstances, troubled by different problems, with different religions, philosophies and political and social assumptions from those of the generation for whom they were written. Yet all this has made little difference. And this is not by chance. There are two levels upon which a book can move us. Every period has, inevitably, its own way of life, its own beliefs, preoccupations, hopes and fears, which, as long as they last, seem to be, and very possibly are, of transcendent importance, and which hence arouse strong, often violent, emotion, but which, when the circumstances which produced them change, are replaced by others and are forgotten. They are like waves upon the surface of the sea. The books in the first class appeal to these surface—and most easily aroused—emotions, but are as ephemeral as the mood which gave them birth. But at the same time, down in the depths, there are the universal and unchanging human passions, problems and aspirations, the same always and everywhere whatever winds may ruffle the surface. The books in the second class penetrate to these depths. The sufferings of an Oedipus or a Hamlet, however much the circumstances, or even the beliefs, which cause them belong to the age in which the play was written, have in themselves nothing to do with fashion or with historical circumstance; they are fundamental to human nature, irrespective of time and place. Now, if you accept (as I think you will) that the greatest literature is that which goes deepest and appeals to what is most universal in man, then I think you will agree that their survival provides *objective* evidence that the books in the second class have a quality of greatness which is lacking in the first.

Nor need we take their greatness on trust. Assuming that we have it in us to respond to great literature, we can as we grow older compare for ourselves the *quality* of our own response to the two classes of books. Most of us in our youth, even though we are at the same time "enjoying" Shakespeare, some of the great novelists and, probably, the more romantic lyrical poetry, go through a phase of responding with something like rapture to the superficially romantic or adventurous second-rate. And meantime many books which we have been told are "great" leave us cold—we are not ready for them. Then there comes a change: as we mature our responses widen and deepen: even the great books which we loved best we now love for a different reason, and, of the rest, one by one we become, so to speak, tuned in to their wavelength; we are ready for them, and they make their full impact. We can now compare the quality and depth of our response to the two groups of books. The "popular" ones may have moved us violently, "carried us away", seemed "perfectly wonderful", but in the "great" books we shall have found a depth, an assurance, a satisfyingness, a calm contentment, which, when we look back, we know was completely lacking in the rush of adolescent emotion produced by the others. However much we "adored" the ephemeral ones (and it is normal, and nothing to be ashamed of, that the young should be indiscriminatingly carried away by what they read), we cannot doubt that were we to return to them we should find them, by comparison with the "great", shallow and shoddy. And further, if we go, when we have reached maturity, from one of the great to almost any new book, even a relatively good one, the difference will be self-evident. Once we have learnt to recognize in ourselves the authentic response to greatness we cannot but be aware of its absence. This alone, without the confirmatory evidence provided by the power of survival, would prove nothing; the impact upon us of the "great" books might be due merely to some subjective kink in ourselves. But when we put the two things together—that not only is there a peculiar quality in our own response to these books but that they have survived innumerable changes of circumstance and fashion, continuing to give pleasure to generation after generation of readers—then it seems to add up to fairly conclusive proof that the difference lies in the books themselves.

Now to return to the critic: although it is true that his judgement on any given book must be based upon his own subjective response, there is an objective test by which we can assess his qualifications: can he recognize greatness where we know that it exists?

The Critic's Qualifications

The man who has read—or attempted to read—Sophocles, Dante, Shakespeare, Tolstoy and the rest and has "seen nothing in any of them" has proved conclusively that he cannot recognize creative genius when he meets with it. If he then sets up for a critic he will be like a colour-blind person setting up as a judge of colour. We can dismiss him from consideration.

This man has taken the test and has failed. But what of one who has never been tested—who for some reason, possibly prejudice due to a faulty education, has not read the attested great, and has confined his reading to contemporary books? This man may have natural taste of a high order—imaginative sensibility and perceptiveness—all the gifts, in fact, required to make him potentially even a great critic. And many of his judgements may be more perceptive than those of a less sensitive though widely-read scholar. But he will have no standard by which to judge; never having experienced the authentic impact of supreme greatness he will not be aware of its absence; he will almost certainly fail to distinguish between the surface waves of topicality and the deeper currents, the ephemeral and the universal.* In virtue of his sensibility he may in any given case be perceptive, but he will be capricious—possibly right, but more probably wrong. He, too, may be dismissed as unqualified.

The critic's essential qualification, both to prove his own capacity for response and in order that he may have a standard by which to judge, is wide and perceptive reading in the great literature of the past. And ideally his taste should be so catholic that, having read every great work, he has responded to the full to all of them. And there have been critics so widely read and so many-sided that little has been beyond their scope.

But such catholicity is rare; temperaments vary: there are born classics, born romantics; some people respond instinctively to the sensuous and emotional, others to the austere and the intellectual, some to formal perfection, others to creative exuberance. We can all, it is true, extend our range and learn at least to admire, even if not to be profoundly moved by, what is alien to our temperaments; we may even, by dint of persevering reading, discover in ourselves latent potentialities for enjoyment until nearly the whole of literature is opened up to us. Nevertheless, in all but the most myriad-minded, blind spots will remain.

But such blind spots do not matter overmuch: what we demand of a critic is not infallibility throughout the whole range of literature, but that *within his own range* he should be a sure guide and should contribute to the utmost to our appreciation and understanding; if he does this he has fulfilled his function; where he fails we can turn to another critic for help. If he is wise he will, of course, recognize his own limitations and confine his judgements to the field in which his sympathies lie. But even if he lacks this wisdom and goes beyond his range the errors which he may make outside his own field in no way invalidate his judgements within it. If these are of superlative quality he remains a great critic, even if a restricted one. Charles Lamb was a born romantic who had no wish to be anything else; not content to say, "I, Charles Lamb, do not like the neo-classical literature of

* In this connection read "The Study of Poetry" in Matthew Arnold's *Essays in Criticism: Second Series.*

the Restoration and the eighteenth century", he assumed that because he failed to respond to it there could be nothing in it to like: the fault must lie in it and not in himself. But this simply means that when we want a just appraisement of the classical period we go elsewhere; it takes nothing from the perceptiveness with which he assesses and illuminates with his poetic imagination the writers of the Elizabethan Age and of the early seventeenth century. So with Samuel Johnson: his verdict on *Lycidas* shows that where pastoral elegy was concerned he was colour blind, but this is totally irrelevant to the greatness of his assessments of *Paradise Lost*, Shakespeare, Pope, Dryden. It is these which put him in the first rank among critics.

There is, it is true, a blind spot which is more serious, and which may itself be caused by the very familiarity with the traditional great which is the critic's essential equipment: the inability to recognize the genius of an innovator who has broken with tradition and has created a new form in which to express his vision. Such innovators were Wordsworth in *Lyrical Ballads* and Gerard Manley Hopkins. It is here that *many-sided reading* is the critic's safeguard. Has he learnt to respond to only one style (as had Wordsworth's critics to the neo-classical) the unorthodoxy of the new form may stand between him and the imaginative content; has he, on the contrary, already discovered in how many ways genius can express itself he will be on his guard against judging by surface orthodoxy and should be able to recognize the authentic impact of greatness even though it may take an unfamiliar form. At worst, being aware of the pitfalls, he can reserve judgement and leave the final verdict to a younger generation of critics whose responses have not become set.

So, to sum up: the wider is a critic's range the better—blind spots are always a fault. But what we demand above all is not the negative merit of absence of errors—they are inevitable, even in the greatest—but that positively the critic should contribute something of unique value to our appreciation of literature and to our ability to recognize, and enjoy, the greatest when we meet with it. And to do this his primary qualification is that he himself should have learnt to respond to the full to the greatest.

The Critic as Interpreter

Already throughout the last section, although writing ostensibly on the critic's qualifications as a judge, I have assumed his further function: interpretation. The two cannot be separated when one comes to write of individual critics: in practice it is in their interpretation that they reveal their judgement.

Yet the two functions are in fact distinct: it is one thing to tell us what is good and what is bad—to separate the sheep from the goats—and quite another to train us to see for ourselves that the sheep are sheep and to enjoy them proportionately. Give an inexperienced reader a list of "The Hundred Best Books" (such lists have been made) and leave him without any guidance as to what to look for in them; a large proportion of them he will find less attractive than current fiction or poetry. Some—the easier novels, lyrical poetry, perhaps drama—may give him great pleasure, though even here he will miss much that a trained sensibility would be aware of. The rest, though he may conscientiously persevere to the end in his pursuit of "culture", will only leave him puzzled as to what other people have seen in them which has led them to be called "great". And this even if potentially he has it in him to be a "good reader". *Great literature needs interpretation.* We may, unaided, get a glimpse, or even more than a glimpse, of the loveliness of a lyric, or the poignancy of a tragic play or story, but a gulf separates us from the intuitions of genius; were it not so it would not be genius. The critic's business is to bridge this gulf. Being himself a man with imaginative perceptions akin to those of his subject, and having by years of concentrated and appreciative reading sensitized himself and trained himself in awareness as no ordinary reader has had the time or the opportunity to do, he then tells that reader what he has discovered in his author, or authors, in such a way that the reader may see it for himself. The critic's methods of interpretation may vary infinitely, but whether he is elucidating a single work or making the most general statements of what to look for in any work of a given kind, always his purpose is the same: to quicken our apprehension of and response to what literature has to say to us so that we may not only know what we ought to read, but get full value out of it when we read it.

The Various Ways in which the Critic Fulfils His Task

(a) *The Critic as Generalizer: The Formulation of Principles*

Every literary work, whether a lyric poem, a play, a novel, or anything else, has its individual qualities: each is unique. Yet, nevertheless, there are certain common characteristics which, in any given class, make for quality or for the reverse. The business of the critic as generalizer is, by watching his own highly trained responses to the various works, good and bad, of any given kind, to isolate and define those qualities which the good have in common so that we may know what to be on the watch for, may recognize it when we meet with it, and notice its absence when it is not there. The first—and he is still the greatest—of all generalizers was Aristotle, in his *Poetics*. Through his own sensitivity, and through his supreme analytic genius, he was able by his study of the individual Greek tragedies to discover the presence in those which satisfied him of certain common factors—a type of hero, a certain kind of plot with "a beginning, a middle and an end"—and, further—his greatest contribution of all—to define the effect of these great tragedies upon his, and our, emotions, imagination and moral being, an effect totally lacking in the lesser ones. He thus, in defining the authentic tragic experience, fulfilled the true function of the critic by directing his readers' attention to the essential so that they might watch for it, recognize it when it was present, and so respond to it to the full. We all of us tend to see only what we are looking for: it was Aristotle who first showed us how, in tragedy, to look for the right thing. And to a lesser extent, too, in comedy and epic, although those he only touched upon in passing.

And when the art of literary criticism was reborn with the

Renaissance it was to such general statements of principle that the critics turned, but, disastrously in the case of the majority, with a total misunderstanding of Aristotle's method and purpose. For they took the business of the critic to be not, as had Aristotle, by observation to discover what in fact was the impact made by any given work, but to turn his statements of what was into rigid and mechanical rules of what ought to be, and appraised any given work not, as he had, by its power to arouse a profound imaginative response, but by a purely mechanical test, "Does it keep the rules?" Thus, much Renaissance and neo-classical criticism is invalidated. It required a critic of exceptional imaginative perceptiveness and independence of mind to dare to trust, as had Aristotle, to his own subjective response, and to say that if any writer had achieved the desired effect by unorthodox means then that only went to show that, right as Aristotle had been about the plays and poems which he knew, there was more than one way of attaining the goal: that the critic's business was not to condemn the "irregular" work but to supplement Aristotle's observations by analysing the new way as he had the old. This is Dryden's greatness: he *knew* that, rules or no rules, Shakespeare moved him more than did any other dramatist; by-passing the whole pedantry of his age he went back to the fundamental question: What is it that Shakespeare has got which makes me *love* him more than I do any "correct" dramatist? And having answered the question he goes on, as would Aristotle himself have done, to extend the definition of great drama so as to include Shakespeare. And Pope, too, though more wedded to the "rules" than was Dryden, knew equally that the business of "rule" was to follow the workings of the imagination and not, conversely, the business of the imagination to keep the rules:

> If, where the rules not far enough extend,
> (*Since rules were made but to promote their end*)
> Some lucky licence answer to the full
> Th'intent propos'd, *that licence is a rule.*

[Pope, *Essay on Criticism*, lines 146–9 (italics mine).]

Dryden and Pope were both working within the classical

tradition. The Romantic Movement brought with it a revolutionary change in poetic sensibility, and a resultant exploration of the very nature of the poetic imagination and its expression in literature. Hence the need for new, and revolutionary, "generalizations". Here the great name is Coleridge, in *Biographia Literaria*; probably no one has done more than has Coleridge to widen and deepen our conception of what poetry is. And, narrower in its range but profound in its insights, Wordsworth's Preface to *Lyrical Ballads*. And Shelley's *A Defence of Poetry*, and, on a lower level but excellent as a summing up of Romantic principles, Hazlitt's essay, *Of Poetry in General*.

The Romantic Period was the great age of inspired criticism. With the Victorians there was a falling off, the major figure being Matthew Arnold, with his attempt to reintroduce a classical discipline as a corrective to romantic extravagance. This re-invigoration of classicism, though a new classicism far removed from eighteenth-century pedantry, has been the main work of T. S. Eliot, first in his essay "Tradition and the Individual Talent" (*Selected Essays*), which, published in 1917, marked a turning point in taste, and in the later volumes *The Use of Poetry and the Use of Criticism* and *What is a Classic?* And, Eliot apart, "generalization" continues today in innumerable specialized studies of some one or other branch of literature; I shall refer to some of them in the course of this book.

(b) *The Critical Appraisement and Elucidation of the Works of Individual Writers*

The earlier critics were all concerned with the formulation of general principles rather than with the study of what differentiated one writer from the rest of his kind. In passing, it is true, they often analysed and passed judgement upon the qualities of many writers and individual works: Aristotle appraises Homer and certain Greek plays; Sidney in his *Apology for Poetry* interpolates the earliest assessment of Spenser, and Dryden in the *Essay of Dramatic Poesy* introduces what is almost certainly the most penetrating and perceptive brief appreciation of Shakespeare which exists. But all these were by the way, introduced in the course of discussing some general truth. But already, with Dryden himself, a new trend was emerging: towards the end of his life, in his Preface to his translations of Virgil, Boccaccio and Chaucer, *On Translating the Poets*, he is concerned not, as his title would suggest, with the art of translation in itself, but to write an appreciation of the three poets—it is Chaucer who in fact takes up the greater part of the essay—for their own sakes. It is modern interpretative criticism—what predominantly, though not exclusively, we expect of the critic today. And by the mid-eighteenth century this new trend was established: though "generalization" continued, the appraisement of individual authors and the analysis of their works had become the critic's main business, reaching its high-water mark in Samuel Johnson's *Preface to Shakespeare* and in the best of his *Lives of the Poets*. Johnson's method is still general in that his aim is to identify the main characteristics of his subject's genius rather than, except to some extent in his annotations of Shakespeare's plays, the detailed line-by-line elucidation of each work. But at his best—as in the greater part of his *Preface to Shakespeare*, and in his *Dryden*, *Pope*, and, superlatively, his *Milton*—his outlines have never been surpassed for balanced judgement and the sureness with which he defines his subject's essential greatness. Johnson's criticism is rational and objective. With the Romantics came an extreme subjectivity—the imaginative re-creation for the reader of what the poetic intuitions of the critic himself had revealed to him in his study of his author—not so much appraisement as *revelation*, the opening up of a new world of meaning in works which the eighteenth century had dispassionately assessed. Again, it was predominantly Shakespeare, but a new Shakespeare, transformed by the romantic sensibility: Coleridge—again the greatest of all—in his *Lectures on Shakespeare*; Lamb, capricious but inspired, in his *The Tragedies of Shakespeare*; Hazlitt's (inferior) *The Characters of Shakespeare's Plays*. The method had its dangers; even Coleridge tended to read into Shakespeare too much of himself. But, though the corrective of greater objectivity was necessary, and has since been provided, the romantic critics wrought a permanent change in the approach to poetry; nothing could ever be the same again.

The Victorians, Matthew Arnold apart, tended to do little but perpetuate the weaknesses rather than the strength of romantic subjectivity. The best of Matthew Arnold's individual studies in *Essays in Criticism*—his *Byron* and *Wordsworth* in particular—combine objectivity with extreme perceptiveness. With the present century, from the 1920's onwards, T. S. Eliot's revival of classical standards in his theoretical writings has been paralleled by a stricter discipline in the assessment of individual works. Here F. R. Leavis has been a major influence. He is a highly controversial figure: to his disciples an inspired prophet, to others a *bête noire*. In reaction against what he saw as an "it's all a matter of taste" subjectivity he has made it his mission to introduce into the practice of criticism puritanically strict professional standards in the place of the dilettantism and amateurism which he sees as the disease of contemporary culture. His faults are exclusiveness and over-dogmatism; what does not fall within his own too narrow definition of excellence is rejected as worthless; his "dethronement of Milton" is notorious. Nevertheless, within his range, when writing of those authors who pass his test, he is one of the most stimulating of living critics, at least on this side of the Atlantic.

But, Leavis apart, it is to my next section that the most significant developments of contemporary criticism belong.

(c) *The Critic as Scholar: Academic Research*

(1) *Historical Research*

Both Samuel Johnson and Coleridge recognized how easy it is to misunderstand the writers of the past for lack of historical knowledge of the circumstances in which they wrote, but in their times the technique of research was still in its infancy. And lesser critics ignored the danger and assumed that, given sufficient perceptiveness, the whole of the world's literature should be equally accessible. But with the growth of the historical sense and the perfecting of research techniques it is now generally accepted that one of the main preoccupations of the critic of literature, at least of that up to the eighteenth century, must be scholarly spade-work in contemporary documents and records. For however universal he may be—however much he may transcend his age—it is now recognized that every writer is, first and foremost, a man of his own day, not only speaking its language (and words are constantly changing their meaning) but working within its social, religious, political and philosophical framework, *and*, most important of all, *taking for granted in his audience or readers the knowledge and presuppositions of the time*. If we do not share this knowledge and these presuppositions but substitute for them those of our own day his whole meaning may be falsified. The business of the critic as scholar is, as far as is possible, to re-create for us the intellectual and emotional climate —even the material setting—which the writer assumed, so that his words may bear for us, again as far as is possible, that meaning and those emotional overtones which their writer intended them to bear. (For the degree to which lack of such knowledge may mislead us read "The Profession of the Critic" in Helen Gardner's *The Business of Criticism.*)

Here again the critic's approach may vary from the most general to the most particular, from, on the one hand, the overall picture of an age to, on the other, the most minute exploration of the personal circumstances, intellectual equipment and idiosyncrasies of a single writer, from that which was the common experience of all men at the time to that which differentiated the one individual genius from all the rest. To the first group belong Tillyard's *The Elizabethan World Picture*, and the various studies of the Elizabethan playhouse which have revealed for the first time how much in the construction of Shakespeare's plays had no abstruse literary significance but was simply due to the fact that that was how they would best come across on the stage for which they were written. At the opposite extreme of particularity is the method known as "explication", the scholarly elucidation, line by line and word by word, of the works of one writer, in the light not only of all that he must have shared with his age but of all that the most exhaustive research can discover of his own personal beliefs, preoccupations and experience. For explication in practice read Helen Gardner's *John Donne; The Divine Poems*.

(2) *Personal Research*

The latter part of the last paragraph has brought us near to what I have called "Personal Research". But however personal the interpretation of a poet such as Donne must be the historical setting still remains all-important; a gulf separates us from the seventeenth century. It is when we come to writers nearer to our own time—to those whose background is relatively familiar to us—that the scholarly critic can, while putting his subject in the setting of his own day, of its beliefs and pre-occupations, yet concentrate his researches almost entirely upon what is particular to himself. Here the classic example is Livingstone Lowes's *The Road to Xanadu*—a classic in its field because, even though he may, as Beer has shown in his recent *Coleridge the Visionary*, have neglected some aspects of Coleridge's philosophical reading, Lowes is almost alone among scholars of his kind in his combination of meticulous detective work with a poetic imagination and intuition through which every fact which he has discovered becomes a source of illumination; setting out to discover, by reading every book which Coleridge's note-books showed that he himself had read, the raw material which the poet's imagination transmuted into the poetry of *The Ancient Mariner* and *Kubla Khan*, he has immeasurably illuminated not only those two poems, but the creative process of the poetic imagination itself. And this is where the academic scholar may fail: it is comparatively rare to find in the same person the capacity for the sheer drudgery—and much of it must be drudgery—of research and the poetic sensibility required to interpret a poem in the light of the facts when they are found. Failing this sensibility the scholar may succeed only in burying a living poem under a mountain of dead information. But where the two gifts are combined the result may be an almost immeasurable "easing, widening and deepening" of our response to poetry.

A Note on "Practical Criticism"

This, the critical method of I. A. Richards, is a highly controversial subject. Carried to its logical conclusion and used to the exclusion of every other method—as it has been by some of the group who call themselves "The New Critics"—it is clearly indefensible. But *if used with common sense*, not to the exclusion of, but as supplementary to, other approaches, it can provide an invaluable discipline in the reading of poetry. I. A. Richards explains his method, and his reasons for advocating it, in his book *Practical Criticism*, published in 1929. To summarize very briefly: he discovered in the course of his teaching at Cambridge that most undergraduates when given a poem to read read not the words printed upon the page but something else which they expected to find; if they knew who wrote the poem they read into it what they had been told that that poet was likely to say; if they did not, they read it as meaning what some other poem with which they were familiar had said on the same subject, or else what they themselves would have said had they been writing the poem. In other words, in each case their response was not to the words in front of them but to something outside the poem of which it reminded them. And their judgement of the poem was equally unrelated to its merits: if they knew the name of the poet they repeated at second hand what they had learnt of that poet's style and quality; if they did not they were all at sea; without the clue of a name they could not distinguish between a good poem and a bad one. This may seem incredible, but not only does my own experience as a teacher confirm it—even my most gifted pupils have from time to time completely reversed the meaning of a poem through inattention to the words—but I myself, after a lifetime of reading, have to be constantly on my guard against such carelessness. The remedy which I. A. Richards suggests is to read the poem in, so to speak, a vacuum, ridding the mind of every preconceived idea as to its probable meaning or quality, forgetting, if you know it, even the name of its author, and concentrating simply and solely upon the words themselves, and then to read and re-read it until every word, every image, every change of metre or rhythm, has made its full impact. From what I have said in the last section the inadequacy of this method as the only approach to poetry is self-evident. But nevertheless, if used side by side with, and not to the exclusion of, scholarly study, it does provide an invaluable discipline for which few readers would not be the better. It must, of course, be practised with common sense: if we know that a poem was written in the seventeenth century naturally we shall read the words in their seventeenth century and not in their modern sense; if we recognize an allusion, again naturally, we shall use any knowledge we may have to get its meaning, and the more such knowledge we have the better. But given this common sense, and given that when we have got all that we can for ourselves out of a poem we go to the scholars and interpretative critics for further help, a course of "practical criticism" can do nothing but good. What is the use of going to others to do for us what we have been too lazy to learn to do for ourselves? This quite apart from the fact that there are many poems, including nearly all contemporary ones, on which no works of scholarship or interpretation exist. If we cannot read these without help we shall not be able to read them at all.

A Postscript on Critics and Reviewers

In the foregoing I may have seemed to suggest that critics are only concerned with the elucidation of the established writers of the past. And many have made this their main, if not their only, preoccupation. But there is another kind of help which criticism can give us: the sorting out from the enormous volume of books published every year of those which are worth reading, and the formulation of the standards by which the majority are rejected and the few pass the test. This is the business of the critic as reviewer, and many of the best critics do turn to reviewing, bringing to the selection and the interpretation of current writing the same absolute standards which they have learnt from the established books of the past. They write for the periodicals whose readers themselves have literary standards and demand the best. But the majority of readers in our semi-literate society ask to be told not what is good in itself, judged as literature, but what they will "enjoy". The reviewers who satisfy this need are no more than commercial journalists; their standard of judgement is not literary merit but popular appeal; they are not, in fact, critics at all, even though they may be so described. But the true critic-reviewer fulfils an indispensable function: not only does he save us the impossible task of discovering for ourselves the books which are worth reading and show us what to look for in them, but, even more important, he can be, so to speak, the growing-point of literary taste, alert to new talent, new developments, new ways of doing the old thing, interpreting for us what, by reason of the unfamiliarity of its form, we might, even if the book should come our way, pass by. Were it not for the perceptiveness of such critics and for their power of exposition no experimental writer would find his public.

CHAPTER II

WHY DO POETS WRITE IN VERSE? SOUND IN POETRY

Why do Poets Write in Verse?

So habitually do poets write in verse that it is not uncommon to find the two words, verse and poetry, used as if they were interchangeable. Yet, of course, "Thirty days hath September . . ." (which is Coleridge's example of verse which is not poetry), or:

> In sixteen hundred and sixty-six
> London burnt like a bundle of sticks

have no more relation to poetry than would the same two statements were they made in prose. And, conversely, the prose translation of the *Song of Solomon* in the Authorized Version of the Bible is as much poetry as is any verse-poem which we read. Whether any piece of writing is poetry or not poetry depends upon its *content* (although, as you will see later, it is true that the poetic content does not become "a poem" until it has found its appropriate form); "verse" and "prose", on the other hand, have reference solely to *form*. The word "verse" simply indicates any piece of writing in which the syllables are so arranged as to produce a recurring rhythm, regardless of what that rhythmical arrangement of words is used to convey to us.* Any piece of writing in which the rhythm does not recur (Free verse apart; see footnote) is prose, again irrespective of its content. Shelley

* "Free verse" complicates the issue; to avoid a digression here I am adding a note at the end of this chapter. For the present ignore it.

says, in his *A Defence of Poetry*, "The distinction between poets and prose writers is a vulgar error"; poets can write in prose, and verse need not be poetry.

Yet, nevertheless, two facts remain: not only have the vast majority of poets, major and minor, chosen verse as their medium, but—even more significantly—every one of the greatest has done so; there is no prose poem in existence which can challenge comparison with the verse-poetry of Homer, Dante, Shakespeare. This cannot be by chance; great poets are not sheep, unthinkingly following the herd; were it possible to transmit the supreme poetic experience in the form of even the most "poetic" of prose some one or other of them would, by experiment, have made the discovery. Hence the verse form must possess some virtue which, when a poet uses it, can transmit "poetry" to us as no prose is able to.

Form and Content

Every work of art contains two elements: the content, what the artist has to say, and the form, how he says it. The form is the externalization in his medium, whether this be paint, musical sound or words, of something which is inside him waiting to get out. The work of art is brought to birth as the content finds its appropriate form; once it is born content and form are inseparable; the content is *in* the form; the form embodies the content; change the form even in the smallest detail, a note in music, a tone in painting, a word in poetry, and the content which it embodies is to that extent changed too. Even for the artist himself content does not completely exist without form; it is only in the process of finding the appropriate form that he knows, except vaguely and nebulously, what it is that he wants to say. A painter hesitating between two tones is not hesitating as to which will best make the picture which is pre-existent in his mind's eye but is in process of discovering what his picture is to be. A composer's work must come to him in musical notes or not at all; the "meaning" is in the notes; until he has found the right ones he has not found his meaning. And so with the poet: he finds the right words, the right images, the right rhythms so that he may tell himself, as well as us, what it is that he has to say; the poem *is* the words.

Prose and Verse

I have already briefly defined the distinction between prose and verse. But before we can go further in discussing the relationship between verse and poetry both definitions need expansion.

I have defined prose as any writing in which the rhythm is non-recurrent. But within this definition, allowing for many border-line cases, prose writings fall into two categories:

(a) *Pure prose.* Here the words will be (or should be—if they are not, the prose is bad) so arranged that when it is read with the natural rise and fall of the speaking voice the stresses will fall on the key words for the meaning. The virtue of pure prose is lucidity; its function is the transmission from the writer's intellect to that of the reader of thought or information; the more faultlessly the placing of the stresses, by accentuating the operative words, clarifies the writer's statements the better is the prose.

(b) *Poetic prose.* Here the arrangement of the stresses serves a double purpose: while still, as in pure prose, accentuating the meaning, their placing at the same time produces a musical rhythm; whereas in pure prose the sound is there for the sake of the sense and the aesthetic pleasure which it gives us is the result of the perfection with which the choice of words and their arrangement conveys that sense to us, in poetic prose *we listen to the sound as sound*; the sound in itself has something to say to us. What this something is will appear when we define poetry.

Verse. Here the function of the stresses (though they must still fall on the key words for the meaning) is to form a recurring rhythmic pattern. The function of this recurrence may be (as in "Thirty days hath September . . .") purely mnemonic; the regular beat makes it easy to learn by heart. But wherever it is used as the vehicle of poetry the rhythm is musical, the distinction between poetic verse and poetic prose lying in the fact that in one the musical rhythm is *patterned*, in the other it is not.

What is Poetry?

"Poetry, in the general sense, is the expression of the imagination" (Shelley, *A Defence of Poetry*). The content of pure prose is facts or ideas directed to our *understanding*; it *tells us* something. Poetry, on the other hand, however much our understanding may be engaged (and it may have profound intellectual content), sets out not primarily to tell us something, but *to make something happen to us*. And what "happens" is the re-creation in our imagination, as a first-hand experience, of something which the poet's imagination has created. When we remember a prose book we remember what the author said in it, or, if it is a novel, what happened to the characters; when we remember a poem we remember something which that poem has made us ourselves see, feel, experience. When we have read Keats's *Ode to a Grecian Urn* what we remember is not that Keats, in the year 1818, saw (in imagination) an urn with certain scenes depicted upon it, that he so felt its unchanging beauty that he underwent the experience of passing out of time into eternity; rather it is that we ourselves, in proportion to our capacity for response, have seen the "still unravish'd bride of quietness", changeless beauty untouched and untouchable by time, and that we in our own persons have, momentarily, passed out of time into timelessness where beauty is the eternal absolute. (And this equally if, when we return to the light of common day our reason questions the philosophical truth of his conclusion.) And if this first-hand imaginative experience has not happened to us then, however clearly our intellect may have grasped the dictionary meaning of the words, what we have read has not been Keats's poem at all.

Lascelles Abercrombie, in his *The Theory of Poetry*, defines what he calls the "inspiration" of poetry as "a unique moment of imaginative experience." Earlier in the chapter he has dismissed the popular misconception that there are certain subjects which in themselves are essentially "poetical"; he then continues, "There is no such thing as a poetical subject: or if you like, all subjects can be poetical; but the poetical thing about them will always be not *what* they are but the way they come to us." Then, having said that "the way they come to us" is the poet's art in the use of language, he proceeds, "Now by *art*, I do not mean simply the clothing of matter in language; I mean as well *something that happened to the matter before that process could begin* . . ." (italics, except *art*, mine). Then comes his definition of the "something" as "*a unique moment of imaginative experience*". All of which is to say that *anything*, never mind what, which has been intensely apprehended by—or, perhaps better, has come alive in—the poet's imagination, can be "poetical", anything which has not been so apprehended—or which has not so come alive—can never make a poem, however "beautiful" or "elevated" it may be. And the poet's business in writing his poem is not to tell us that this "moment of imaginative experience" has happened to him, but to make it happen to us as well.* Poetry, in Shelley's words, "in the general sense, is the expression of the imagination", and it is with our *imagination* that we must apprehend it—or not at all.

At last we are within sight of answering the question with which this chapter began. But it now needs re-stating in other words: What is there in the nature of verse which helps the poet to transmit his imaginative experience to the reader as prose cannot? Why is prose predominantly the vehicle of "telling about", verse of re-creation?

Words used solely in their dictionary meaning and arranged in their grammatical order can generally only tell us about something. There are, it is true, exceptions; they can be used to form

* The statement "There is no such thing as a poetical subject" needs further expansion, but to expand it here would lead us away from the present question, the relationship between verse and poetry. I am therefore adding a note at the end of this chapter.

images—the theme of the next chapter—or they can evoke overtones by association. But as a general rule this statement holds good: each word stands for some object, action or intellectual concept; their function is to communicate information or ideas from one mind to another. It is true that they can arouse intense emotion in us if the information which they give us is painful or pleasant, or if they promise something which we desire or threaten something which we fear. But this is because they communicate to us emotion-producing facts; the emotion which we feel is our own, the product of those facts. This seems to be true even in the case of the majority of great novels: the novelist has imagined the scene intensely and may have felt deep emotion as he wrote, but nevertheless it is the situation which he describes—what he tell us—that arouses emotion in us;* we sympathize with—are moved by—the joys and sorrows of the characters in the novel, but they remain *theirs*, something outside ourselves. Their experiences never become our own as does Keats's when we read the *Grecian Urn*.

But there is an art which, without the use of words at all, can *by sound alone* thus transmit to and reproduce in our imagination the artist's "meaning": music. The only difference between one musical composition and another—between Beethoven's Fifth Symphony and his Seventh, or between either of these and anything of Bach or Mozart or of any other composer—is in the different quality and arrangement of the musical notes. Yet no two have the same "meaning"; each by communicating directly through the ear with some deep level of our consciousness produces in us a totally different response, transmitting to us, in proportion as our ear is trained to hear, what the composer (as interpreted by the executant) has to "say". And this, I repeat, *by the arrangement of sounds alone*.

* A great novel is, of course, the work of the creative imagination, and thus covered by Shelley's definition of "poetry *in general*". But Shelley himself in his *Defence of Poetry* narrows his definition when he comes to poetry in the commonly accepted sense of the word, and, although I have not space here to develop the point, I believe that there is a difference in kind between the poetic imagination and the creative power of the novelist.

The poet combines two arts, the art of using words as words to communicate meaning, and the art of so choosing and arranging them that their sounds may make a rhythmic musical pattern which speaks directly through the ear to the imagination as do the notes in music.

Why a Recurring Rhythm?

So—musical sound. But if this is all the poet needs why not poetic prose? What is gained by the use of the recurring rhythm of verse?

Verse performs two main functions. First comes a matter of empirical observation: a recurring rhythm can in fact release profound, or even violent, emotion. On the most primitive level, far removed from that of the poet, there is the sound of the tom-tom; those who have heard it in the African bush speak with something like terror of its fear-provoking power. And this power is irrational; the hearer may be in no personal danger; it is the sound in itself which has aroused his fear. So with the rhythmic beat of dance music, whether of the savage war-dance or of the contemporary "rhythm" which arouses the young to near-frenzy. One could add examples indefinitely. And in every case one would find that not only is emotion as such released, but a specific emotion—fear, belligerency, erotic passion, or whatever it may be—according to the pattern made by the recurring beats. This release of raw primitive passion is, of course, the very antithesis of the poet's aim, yet, though for a very different purpose, it is this unique power of a repetitive rhythm to penetrate directly to the emotions, and through them to the imagination, *and to condition the nature of the response*, that he uses when he writes in verse.

But this, the release of emotion, is only the beginning: passion needs not only to be released, but *to be controlled and ordered and directed towards a meaningful end.* That is the function of the artist, whatever be his medium. Life is a thing of bits and pieces, of disorder and disunity; human nature craves for unity, for an ordered comprehensible wholeness. The profound aesthetic satisfaction which we receive from all great art is just this: the disordered raw material of life has been mastered and controlled and a pattern imposed upon it; the warring elements have been unified into harmony—even though it may be a tragic harmony; what was formless has been given shape and moulded into wholeness. And verse, by its ordered pattern, gives us just this sense of control and mastery. Not only our ear, but our deep-seated desire for order, for pattern, is satisfied as line after line falls into place at the poet's will; the whole is a rhythmic unity, with a beginning, a middle and an end.

And this rhythmic unity—this rounded-off pattern—is far more than a matter of form alone; in the very process of shaping his verse the poet has been forced to shape his material; the patterned form is the outward expression of an inner patterning of the material itself which in its turn has conditioned the metrical pattern of the verse. The discipline of writing verse has organized, given unity to, not only the words, but the content. In a sense one may even say that the verse form itself has become a part of the content; its very ordered shapeliness tells us something that the words do not: that the poet has reached a state of equilibrium in which he can contemplate his experience and see it as a whole. And this is why the pattern of the verse itself gives us such profound pleasure.

So, to sum up: the recurring rhythm of verse not only stirs the emotions and, through them, the imagination, by penetrating to the deeper levels of consciousness, but at the same time it orders and controls the emotions so aroused and gives to the finished poem—not only to its form but to its content—an aesthetically satisfying pattern and unity.

"The Sound must seem the Echo to the Sense"

So much for the answer to the question at the head of this chapter. And if "verse" were just "verse", if the choice were merely between *a* recurring rhythm and a non-recurring one, this would be all there was to be said. But (a) the poet must choose not only *a* verse form but the one with the right rhythmic pattern to transmit his content, and (b), once he has chosen it its "transmitting" power will depend upon *what he does with the sounds within its framework*. (a) is, I think, obvious: the quick movement of the octosyllabic couplet, the slower continuity of blank verse, the slow-moving self-contained completeness of the Spenserean stanza or the succession of four-line units in the ballad form clearly are not interchangeable; imagine *Paradise Lost* written in ballad metre or *The Ancient Mariner* in blank verse; the incompatibility between form and content is self-evident.

But it is not enough to choose the right metre; the number of metres is limited, the content of no two poems is the same. Did all blank verse sound alike Macbeth's soliloquies, *Paradise Lost* and Wordsworth's *Prelude* would have the same musical pattern and hence their sound would say the same thing to our imaginations. And even within the range of one poet's use of his medium, the rhythmic pattern of Macbeth's "Is this a dagger . . ." and 'Tomorrow and tomorrow and tomorrow", of Milton's Hell and his Paradise, of Wordsworth's most exalted and most homely passages, would be indistinguishable—all would have the same five beats to a line and nothing more. Were the choice of verse form all, all sonnets would sound alike: Wordsworth could not have heard Petrarch's "lute", Tasso's "pipe" nor Milton's "trumpet"; the impact upon us of the Spenserean stanzas of *The Faerie Queene*, *The Eve of St. Agnes* and *Adonais* would be the same.

The poet's business, once he has chosen his appropriate metre, is to use it as an ordered framework *within which he writes his own music*. And his own music lies in the lightening or adding weight to, or even shifting, the stresses, and in the sound quality of the words which he uses. Some words are heavy and slow-moving, others light and quick; they may have velvety softness or metallic sharpness; the resonance of an organ or the thinness of a robin's song; they may be harsh, discordant (and discord has its place when the sense demands it), or smoothly mellifluous. Given the metrical framework of his verse form, it is of these sounds that the poet's music is made.

And if as we read we fail to hear these sounds, then we shall equally fail to respond to the sense which the poet has used them to transmit to us. Hence the necessity for ear-training. And this, in fact, is the moral of this chapter.

Ear-training

Ear-training is as essential to the reader of poetry as it is to the student of music, yet few who have "done" poetry as an examination subject have been taught even the first elements of it. The untrained ear will, it is true, pick up the general pattern of the rhythm; it may be vaguely aware of a speeding up or of a retarding of the movement, of the sweetness of certain lines, of the incantatory power of certain passages. But the emotional effect will be *generalized*; not being on the alert, the ear will literally not have heard the changes in the sound pattern in which the poet has embodied, not *a* "poetical" mood, but the *specific* "meaning" which is his intention.

> 'Tis not enough no harshness give offence;
> The sound must seem the Echo to the sense.

And that means *every* sound; in proportion to the poet's technical skill (and lacking such skill he has, whatever his intention, failed as a poet), not a variation of sound can escape us without some part of his "meaning" being lost. Miss the deep resonance of one line and the transition to airy lightness in the next, the soft smoothness of alliterating "f"s and "v"s and "th"s, or the harshness of "k"s and (hard) "g"s, the weight of a spondee, or the lightness of a "light ending", and you will, to that extent, have missed what the poet has to say.

To train the ear two things are necessary: we must *learn to listen* and we must learn *what to listen for*. The two disciplines must proceed concurrently; the first involves a change in our reading habits, the second the study of prosody.

Learning to listen. Our whole education tends to train us to read by eye alone. The quicker the eye registers the symbols printed on the page and transmits them to the brain to be translated into mental concepts the better readers we are considered to be. And so we are if what we are reading is what De Quincey called "the Literature of Knowledge", where sense is everything and sound (except in so far as the stresses lead us to identify the operative words) is nothing. But if we are to read poetry the first step must be to break this habit. My own method of breaking the "eye-habit" and acquiring the "ear-habit"—other people might suggest another—is, as I read, to form every word with my mouth as if I were speaking it aloud, and, as I do so, to listen in imagination to the sounds which my mouth forms. Try it, and see if it helps you. The first effect will be a difference of speed. It takes the eye alone no longer to register a long syllable than a short one—the first syllable, say, of "holy" than that of "holly"—it will race over each equally. But if it has to wait until the mouth has formed each syllable before going on to the next then inevitably our reading will be slowed down or speeded up in proportion to the sound-length of the words. The second effect is more complex; the quality of the sounds, soft, hard, light, heavy and the rest, is as important as their duration; the movements of our mouths in making them are, from a life-time of habit, psychologically associated with hearing; if while forming them we concentrate our attention upon, in imagination, listening to what we are saying these movements will in themselves help to reproduce in our ear the sounds with which each is associated. At a first attempt you may find that the effort of attending to what your mouth is doing takes your mind off what you are reading, but if you continue until the habit becomes second nature I think you will find that "hearing" has become automatic.

But even so, the sounds which you hear will only be those which you yourself would enunciate were you reading the poem aloud. They will be far nearer to the poet's intention than the eye-reader's soundlessness, but almost certainly, because your ear is still not fully trained, you will introduce distortions, and quite certainly you will miss many subtleties of movement, volume and tone of which a trained and perceptive reader would be aware. My second suggestion for ear-training is that you should miss no opportunity of hearing poetry *well* read. I stress "well"; good readers of poetry are few and far between and the rest will do you more harm than good. There are—imaginative response to the content of the poem apart—two requirements in a reader of poetry: an instructed feeling for the sound of verse and a voice which is able to reproduce it. Of these the first is most likely to be found in poets themselves, and if they have the second as well then they may well be the best interpreters, if not of all poetry, at least of their own. And there are now plenty of opportunities of hearing contemporary poets reading their own verse, both on records and on the Third Programme. Listen, if you can, to the record (it is a very old one) of T. S. Eliot's reading of *The Four Quartets*; not only will the sounds form themselves into a pattern, which however often you may have read the poems to yourself, will in itself be a revelation, but, just because the "sense" is so perfectly echoed by the sound, the meaning will come home to you as it never has before. Poets apart, there are actors, and many do broadcast poetry, again generally on the Third. But here you must be selective; the trouble with many actors is that, although their voices are trained, they have been trained primarily to speak colloquial prose, and that "dramatically"; the words are not trusted to make their own impact but "played up" as the vehicle of the actor's interpretation of his part. The actor-readers to watch for are those who have learnt their art in the school of verse drama, first and foremost among them Sir John Gielgud. Never miss an opportunity of hearing him speak verse, whether on the stage or on the air. One of the highlights of my memories of broadcasting is his reading of *The Ancient Mariner*; perhaps the B.B.C. may some day re-broadcast a recording of it. The reading was charged with poetic passion, but the passion was transmitted not through something superimposed upon the words by the reader, but simply by the perfect production of every rhythm, every modulation, every rise and fall in volume, of the verse itself. In proportion as a reader approaches to this standard he is a good reader of poetry.

What to listen for; Prosody. But to listen uninstructedly is not enough; we must listen with understanding; the sound pattern of verse is made up of often intricate combinations of rhythmic units, and unless the ear is on the alert for these units and recognizes them when they come, it will, quite literally, fail to hear them, as the uninstructed listener to music will fail to hear anything but the general outline of any composition he may listen to. And this alertness and recognition can only come through a knowledge of prosody. Only the habit of analysing the rhythm of any line of verse into its component units—iambs, trochees and the rest—can discipline our ears to distinguish between one verse pattern and another and to hear the variations which the poet has introduced into it so that the sound may echo the sense.

But the study of prosody can help us only on two conditions: (1) We must treat it as a means to an end and not as an end in itself, and (2) the principles must be correctly taught.

(1) The ultimate end is not to scan a line of verse, naming each foot, or to identify a verse form, and to stop there. Yet this is all that many people have been taught to do. If we set out to do no more than this, we might as well occupy ourselves doing a crossword puzzle. We must indeed go through a period of mere naming, of identification, but its purpose is not achieved until, by dint of the intelligent concentration of the attention required for naming, our ear has learnt automatically to recognize the sound units, and to respond to their sound *as sound.* The process of hearing and naming is one of continuous give and take. First we must hear, for until we hear at least something we shall have nothing to scan; the discipline of scansion will then alert our ears to more accurate hearing; that improved hearing will in its turn show us niceties which our untrained ear had missed; these in their turn will need analysis. And so the process will go on. And even to the end we shall constantly go back and analyse the

pattern of a line which we have read to discover how the poet has achieved his effect, as the instructed listener to music will return to the score to discover the notes of which what he has heard is made up. But always the analysis is not for its own sake but for the purpose of alerting our ear to respond with even greater exactitude to the subtleties of the poet's technique.

(2) *The principles of prosody.* Here comes a difficulty. To explain the rules of prosody requires a book rather than a few paragraphs, yet I know of no elementary introduction which states the principles correctly; the scholarly studies are too advanced for beginners. All that I can do is to give you some suggestions which will save you from being misled by whatever book you may use.

For the names of the feet which are the units of verse you can, if you do not already know them, go to a school textbook or look up the five feet used in English verse—the iamb, trochee, anapaest, dactyl and spondee—in the section "Technical Terms" in Fowler's *Modern English Usage*. So with the various verse forms, the iambic pentameter, alexandrine, octosyllabic couplet, heroic couplet, blank verse, the Spenserean stanza, *ottava rima*, the Petrarchan and Shakespearean sonnet forms and the rest. This will give you a working knowledge of the terminology and enable you to identify the metre in which any poem is written.

But to identify the metre, though essential, is not enough; what matters is what the poet has done with it. And it is here that a textbook—or Fowler—is likely to mislead you: the examples of scansion which are given are likely to be so mechanical, if not actually faulty, as to distort rather than to elucidate the pattern of the verse, and so to corrupt rather than to sensitize your ear. At this point, if you are not to be led astray, you will need to remember the two following distinctions. If you bear them in mind when practising scansion, although you will still have much to learn, you will at least be working on the right principles and should have nothing to unlearn when you arrive at more advanced study.

(1) *"Irregularity": "Variation"*

Most elementary textbooks will tell you, e.g., that an iambic pentameter—the line unit of blank verse, the heroic couplet, the sonnet—consists of five iambs. They then, their authors knowing perfectly well that the majority of iambic pentameters do nothing of the sort, introduce the word "irregularity": whenever Milton or Shakespeare varies the beat of the five iambs by substituting a foot of a different kind, that line is "irregular". Now, the word "irregular" means "contrary to rule"; its use in this context implies that there is a rule that every iambic pentameter should consist of five iambs, and that in breaking it Milton or Shakespeare has written faultily. In fact, *no such rule exists, or can exist*, for if it did its observance would mean that the sound (a monotonous repetition of five "tee-tums" in every line) could not conceivably echo the sense, and so would defeat the poet's aim in writing in verse. (This apart from the fact that a long poem so written would inevitably send us to sleep.) There is a rule, but a very different one: a poem written in iambic pentameters must contain a sufficient number of lines of five iambs to keep going in the ear a recurrent rhythmic beat, and no line must vary so much from the norm as not to fit into this framework; if it does we say that that line "does not scan". But within this framework the poet not only may, but *must*, introduce variations, trochees, spondees, anapaests, feminine endings—*and it is in the use of these variations that his skill as a metrist consists*. Far from writing "irregularly"—contrary to rule—he is, in introducing them, obeying the rules of his art. Read any one of Shakespeare's sonnets, following the natural rhythm of the words and being careful not to impose upon them the succession of "tee-tums" which the textbook definition of the iambic pentameter may have led you to expect; the effect will be one of perfect "regularity", of an uninterrupted rhythmic flow. Then re-read it line by line, preserving the stresses which came naturally to you in your first reading, and scan each line—divide it into its component feet and mark the stresses. You will find that there are few lines which do not contain at least one trochee or spondee or other variation. And when you come to re-read the sonnet as a whole, letting its sound make its full impact upon your imagination, you will discover that it is in these variations—in the weight of the spondees, the reversal of rhythm in the trochees, and the rest—that the "sense" is embodied. This relating of sound to sense takes considerable knowledge and experience; at a first attempt much will escape you. But, to turn from Shakespeare to Milton, even a beginner's ear should, if on the alert, be able to hear the slow, heavy, tedious, long-drawn-out toiling of the exploring fallen angels in the three spondees of the last line of this passage from *Paradise Lost:*

> . . . through many a dark and drearie Vaile
> They pass'd, and many a Region dolorous,
> O're many a Frozen, many a Fierie Alpe,
> *Rocks, Caves, Lakes, Fens, Bogs, Dens* and shades of Deathe . . .

To describe this line as "contrary to rule" betrays ignorance of the first elements of prosody. It exemplifies the rule as only the work of a great metrist can.

For the sake of simplicity I have spoken only of the iambic pentameter. But of course the same principle applies to every metre: whatever verse form the poet may choose it is in his variations upon it that he shows his metrical skill; expect them, listen for them, learn to recognize them when they come.

(2) *Quantity: Stress*

Many elementary books, and even some old-fashioned scholarly ones, describe the feet in English verse in terms of "short" and "long"; an iamb is said to be short-long (and marked (∪ –), a trochee long-short (– ∪), and so with the rest. This is the correct terminology for classical metres, but not for English, for the principles of classical and English prosody are not the same. Greek and Latin verse are quantitative, that is to say the rhythm is formed by the alternation of long and short syllables, the long syllable, if the verse is correctly spoken, taking half as long again to say as the short, *stress being ignored*. But the rhythm of English verse is formed, not quantitatively, but by recurring *stresses*, the syllable which would be short in a classical metre being unstressed, that which would be long stressed, *regardless of the length of the syllable*. The use of the words "long" and "short" in describing English metres might not matter (although the misuse of words always leads to confused thinking) if we could, in analysing the rhythm of any given line, ignore the length of the syllables. But we cannot: some of the poet's subtlest effects are achieved by, while observing the stress pattern, interweaving with it another pattern of long and short syllables, slowing down, perhaps, or giving weight to, a line by a predominance of long syllables, or speeding it up or lightening it by a predominance of short ones. Now, if you have begun by describing the stressed syllables as long and the unstressed as short, what are you to say if you find a short syllable in a stressed position? "In the second and third feet the long syllable is short"? But nothing can be both long and short at the same time. And it is not only a matter of terminology; the words we use condition our thinking: call the stresses stresses, as they are, and you will listen for stresses; keep the words "long" and "short" in reserve for their proper purpose, and you will not forget to listen for the slowing down or speeding up, the weight or lightness, which result from the length of the syllables within the stress pattern. Even the symbols ∪ – should be avoided; not only are they inaccurate, as indicating quantity, but they make no distinction between a heavy stress and a light one, and on this difference the rhythm of a line may depend. Unfortunately, no system of notation exists by which the exact weight of each stress can be indicated, but we can at least distinguish between heavy and light by the use of the accents \ and /. Compare these two possible iambic pentameters:

– \ – \ – \ – / – / has a rising rhythm, and

– / – / – / – \ – \ has a falling one. If the symbols ∪ – had been used the two would be indistinguishable.

A Note on Free Verse

Free verse, of course, has not a regularly recurring rhythm. In his desire to make the sound more exactly echo the sense than he believes possible within the limits of the traditional metres, the poet holds himself free, not only to introduce variations into the recurring rhythms of his lines, but to vary the length and the metrical pattern of the lines themselves, improvising as he goes along. Yet free verse can, if the writer is a skilled enough metrist, fulfil the function of verse—the function of giving a rhythmic structure to the poem, of turning it into a patterned unity in which each line falls into place as an organic part of an ordered rounded-off whole. What distinguishes successful free verse from poetic prose—apart from the fact that in the printing it is cut up into lines instead of being printed continuously—is that, whereas in prose the rhythmic unit is the sentence, in free verse, as in all verse, it is *the line*. No two lines may be alike, but each is *heard as a unit*, line being added to line until the shape of the poem is complete. If when we read free verse there is nothing but the printing to tell us where one line ends and the next begins the writer has failed; he has written not verse but prose arbitrarily cut up to make it look "poetic". And, contrary to common opinion, success is far more difficult than in the writing of traditional verse, for the poet has nothing but his ear to guide him; he has no rules, no models; if his ear fails him he is lost; an inexperienced writer embarks upon it at his peril. But given in the poet a highly trained ear, great metrical skill and self-discipline sufficient to take the place of the external discipline of the traditional verse forms, free verse can qualify as verse and fulfil its functions.

Note 2. "There is no such thing as a poetical subject"

In my section "What is Poetry?" all that I was concerned with was to make it clear that it is not the subject in itself but what the poet's imagination has done to it which makes it "poetical".

To have developed the matter more fully would have led away from the question at issue, the relationship between poetry and verse. But from the point of view of the approach to poetry as such—of what one is to look for in it—there is more to be said.

First, the matter of "beauty" in poetry. A common assumption is that (a) the business of poetry is to be "beautiful" and (b) to be beautiful it must have a "beautiful" subject. As to (a), that depends upon what one means by "beauty"; I will return to it later; before we can decide in what sense, if any, poetry must be beautiful we must dispose of (b). And the matter is, of course, already disposed of by implication in Lascelles Abercrombie's "There is no such thing as a poetical subject: or, if you like *all subjects can be poetical* . . ." (italics mine). But so strong is the prejudice in favour of "beauty", in the commonly accepted sense of the word, that we cannot leave it at that. In the first draft of my expansion of this statement on page 25, I wrote, "All of which is to say, anything, *never mind how apparently trivial or even sordid*, which has been intensely apprehended . . .", but, not wishing at that point to confuse the issue by raising the question of beauty or ugliness, I crossed out the italicized words, and substituted, "never mind what". I now restore the missing words. Beauty or ugliness *in the subject* has no bearing upon the ultimate beauty of the poem: all that matters is the intensity with which either has been apprehended by, and has come alive in, the poet's imagination—and, of course, found its expression in words. And evil, the ugly, the grotesque, can be, and in certain poets are, apprehended with as great poetic intensity as beauty. The function of poetry is not to provide a romantic escape from evil into a world of lovely make-believe, but to intensify our awareness of the whole of reality—the reality of beauty, of course—that goes without saying—but equally of evil, of the ugly, and by the transmuting power of the imagination to give it a meaning, a significance, which constitutes "poetic beauty". If beauty of subject is the mark of poetry, what of Shakespeare's sonnet "The expense of spirit in a waste of shame / Is lust in action . . ."? It is a distillation of a mood of utter revulsion against the degradation of what in itself is ugly, lust. Even the words are not "beautiful" in the accepted sense; they match the meaning. Yet its impact upon the imagination surpasses in depth and intensity that of any of his "beauty" sonnets; it is the greatest sonnet he wrote, the only one which reveals the Shakespeare of the great tragedies. Or what is "beautiful" in Browning's *Soliloquy in a Spanish Cloister*? Yet it is poetry, even if not of the highest order; only the poetic imagination could have made it, and to read it is a poetic experience. If you want to have the point put simply, and convincingly, that a superficially "beautiful" poem may not be poetry, and a superficially unbeautiful one may be, read the chapter "When is a Poem not a Poem?" in Cecil Day Lewis's *Poetry for You*.

Now for (a): granted that the subject of a poem need not in itself be beautiful, in what sense, if any, must the finished poem be so? Not, certainly, in the dressing up of an ugly subject in conventionally beautiful words: Donne would not have improved his line, "Or snorted we in the Seven Sleepers' den" by substituting a more pleasing word for "snorted", or, for that matter, by smoothing out the rhythm of the line; his whole point is the ugliness of life without love; the ugliness of the word, and of the versification, is intentional. Nor would Shakespeare have increased the poetic beauty of his sonnet by the use of mellifluous and decorative language; his whole intention would have been falsified. Nor, of course, must the ugliness of the subject itself be played down or diluted; the business of poetry is not to dilute but to intensify.

The answer to the question depends upon our definition of "beauty". In its commonly accepted use it means something which is pleasing to the eye or ear. A rose is "beautiful", and so is a woman with faultless features, complexion and figure; so is the nightingale's song. There is no beauty in a slag heap, a deformed dwarf, or in the sound of a pneumatic drill. This is what we mean by beauty—and its reverse—in "real life". But when applied to the arts—if we use it at all, and so much is it associated in our minds with its "real life" meaning that to avoid ambiguity it is often better not to use it—the word means something different: that which gives aesthetic pleasure. And the specific aesthetic pleasure which the arts give us lies in our pleasurable response to the perfect formal expression of what the artist's vision has given him to express. This expression may—and in the majority of cases does—possess beauty in the every-day sense of the word, but even so it is our feeling for the absolute *rightness* with which form embodies content—the perfect command of the artist over his material—which is the essence of our pleasure, and which differentiates our response to a work of art from our pleasure in "natural" beauty. In nature we are pleased by the thing in itself; in art by what the moulding human spirit has done to it. If by "poetic beauty" we mean this—the perfection with which the form embodies the poet's vision and transmits it to us alive and whole—then every poem must have beauty. But not in the common sense of the word.

A second, though perhaps a less fundamental point: thought, and the play of intellect, in poetry. A romantic heresy—though one not subscribed to by the greatest romantics—is that, because poetry must be addressed to the emotions, thought, as such, can play no part in it; that Dryden and Pope wrote mere versified prose, and that even in *Paradise Lost* there are two separable strands, the poetry and the theology. It is true that pure cerebration can never make poetry. *But thought can be imagined*: thinking in itself can be an intellectual adventure charged with passion, as an electric flex is charged with power; when this happens the pursuit of truth, and its discovery, can become as much an "imaginative experience" as falling in love; it is, in fact, a form of falling in love: the poet is in love with truth, and hence it is as much a "poetic subject" as is that of a love-lyric.

CHAPTER III

IMAGERY

So MUCH for the sound of poetry. But it is not by the sound alone that the poet transmits his imaginative experience to us; unlike the musician's notes, his words have meaning. The total effect comes of the perfect union of sound and sense; what the words say to us must speak as directly to our imagination as do their sounds. And this they can do most supremely when they are used to form sensuous images. It is—sound apart—in his imagery most of all that the poet, rather than "telling us something", makes something happen to us. Aristotle in the *Poetics* (Bywater's translation, p. 78), speaking of the poet's use of words, says, "*But the greatest thing of all is to be a master of metaphor*. It is the only thing which cannot be learnt from others, and it is also a sign of genius. . . ." And Shelley, in *A Defence of Poetry*, ranks together metaphor and rhythm as the two essentials of poetry; having spoken of melody, harmony and rhythm, he then says, "Their [the poets'] language is vitally metaphorical. . . ." And each goes on to give the same reason; to that we will return later.

The word "image", of course, originally meant a visual picture. But in the language of literary criticism its meaning has been both extended and restricted: extended in that its use is no longer confined to the visual but now includes the calling up in the imagination of an impression made upon any of the five senses, hearing, taste, touch and smell as well as sight, but restricted in that—at least in its form "imagery"—it is now generally limited to such sensuous impressions when they are used to make metaphors or similes. So when we speak of imagery we exclude direct description however visual (though, as you will see later, there is sometimes a case to be made for its inclusion), and we include all metaphors and similes, to whichever of the five senses they may be addressed.

Metaphor and Simile

The type of the poetic image is the *metaphor*. The function of a metaphor is to turn one thing into another by transferring certain characteristics of the metaphorical object to the literal one, while yet never letting us forget that the literal object is itself. A is spoken of not as being *like* B; *it has become B*; when Collins says,

> Spring, with dewy fingers cold,
> Returns to deck their hallow'd mould. . . .

he is not telling us that Spring is *like* a being with cold dewy fingers placing flowers upon a grave: Spring *is* the being, and the being *is* Spring.

A simile does grammatically set two things side by side and tell us that they are alike:

> O my luve's *like* a red red rose
> That's newly sprung in June. . . .

And a prose simile does in fact set two things side by side and asks our intellects to compare them. But a poetic simile which does no more than this has failed: it has succeeded only if its impact upon the imagination is that of a metaphor, if, as has happened with Burn's "luve", although the two objects are formally distinct, certain essential elements of the second are seen as belonging to the first. I will illustrate this more fully as we go on; for the present the point to remember is that, whether the grammatical form is that of simile or metaphor, the purpose of the image is that, by a process of *transference*, we should see one thing as having taken to itself something of another.

Why Imagery?

The purpose of an image is to speak directly to the imagination through one or more of the five senses. Milton—and he practised what he preached: *Paradise Lost,* for all its intellectual and religious content is one of the most sensuous poems in the English language—said that poetry must be "simple, *sensuous* and passionate". And Shakespeare, in one of the few passages in his plays where he seems to be speaking in his own person, as a poet, through a character (Theseus, in *A Midsummer Night's Dream*), says:

> . . . As imagination *bodies forth*
> The forms of things unknown, the poet's pen
> Turns them *to shapes,* and gives to airy nothings
> A local habitation and a name. . . .

What the poet has to say to us must come to us *in a body,* a concrete form, *a shape* visible to the eye; "airy nothings", "forms of things unknown" are, until they are "bodied forth", no stuff for poetry.

I will now make three dogmatic statements followed by a conclusion which, if the statements are accepted, you will, I think, agree follows logically from them; I will then go on to justify the statements. (1) poetry is addressed to the imagination; (2) abstract concepts address themselves solely to the intellect; (3) all that stirs the imagination and the emotions comes to us through one or more of the five senses. *Therefore* poetry must be sensuous.

You have, I hope, already accepted (1); it is (2) and (3) which you will probably question: "Abstract concepts address themselves solely to the intellect", "All that stirs the imagination and the emotions comes to us through one or more of the five senses." What then of such words as "love", "beauty", "death"? They are abstract nouns and yet highly emotive. But would any of them arouse the slighest tremor of emotion did they not remind us of some experience which in the first instance came to us through sight, hearing and the rest? *We do not love in the abstract: we love a person*—and a person whom our eyes have seen, whose voice our ears have heard, and who, probably, we have touched in an embrace; it is through seeing, hearing, perhaps touching, that the experience of love has come to us. Had we only learnt the dictionary definition of the word, or even studied a philosophical disquisition on its meaning, we might *reason* about it till the end of time, but emotion and imagination would remain untouched. So with "beauty"; we might be able to define it as "that which gives aesthetic pleasure", but had we never experienced that pleasure through seeing a beautiful sight, hearing a beautiful sound, smelling a beautiful scent, it would remain a mere intellectual concept. The word "death", too, only moves us in proportion as we have either experienced, or at least visualized in imagination, death in the concrete, an individual physical body dying. Though formally abstract, these and all other like terms stir our imaginations only in proportion as they have ceased to be abstractions; it is not the abstract concept itself but the concrete and sensuous experiences which each calls up in our memory which stirs the emotions. So I think we can conclude that poetry, if it is to appeal to the imagination, must be sensuous.

And, further, the more exact, the more particularized, is the sensuous impression the greater will be its impact. This is where the emotive-abstract words such as "love", "beauty", fail. Their sensuous associations are diffused, generalized; lazy poets are content to use them; good ones need something more specific. Suppose that Keats had begun his *Grecian Urn* with its conclusion: "Beauty is truth, truth beauty", and had continued throughout the Ode to expand his thought in abstract terms, what impact other than, perhaps, a vague sense of "the beautiful" would the verses have upon us? What he has done is, before using the word "beauty", to fill it with specific meaning by, through the length of four stanzas, letting us *look at* one individual beautiful object. Even in the opening lines of *Endymion* it is "a *thing* of beauty", and not beauty in the abstract, which is "a joy for ever", and by the fourth line he has passed to concrete imagery.

So the first—and the simplest—function of imagery is thus *to embody the abstract in sensuous form*. Here are some examples so that you can compare for yourselves the impact on your imagination of the image and of the abstract statement which it embodies.

First, Shirley's "Death *lays his icy hand on kings*". What Shirley is telling us is that "even kings do not escape death"; put like this its impact is practically nil; we know it already; it remains a familiar truism and nothing more. But when we see the picture, death no longer an abstraction but given "a body"—a figure, sinister, macabre—and when we feel the touch of the icy hand which he lays upon the king we no longer know the fact only theoretically, as something remote from our experience: *we have seen it and felt it*; the image remains, stamped permanently upon our memory. Then compare the abstract "All joys are transitory" with Keats's

> Joy, whose hand is ever at his lips
> Bidding adieu . . .

or Shelley's

> Life, like a dome of many coloured glass,
> Stains the white radiance of eternity

with the philosophical statement: "In the Eternal Absolute all is undifferentiated oneness; the variety of appearances which we know exists only in time." And look at Wordsworth's Sonnet to Milton:

> England hath need of thee; she is *a fen*
> *Of stagnant waters* . . .

where England's moral corruption and apathy have been turned into a picture of physical corruption and stagnation. Again, in the same sonnet:

> Thy soul was *like a star and dwelt apart*. . . .

Here is purity, radiance, aloneness, "aboveness": the picture of the night sky infinitely remote, with the one solitary light-giving star which embodies in itself the spiritual meaning which Milton had for Wordsworth. And, as a final example, in Marvell's "To His Coy Mistress", there is an image so complex that it defies translation into abstract terms:

> Let us roll our strength and all
> Our sweetness up into one ball.
> And tear our pleasures with rough strife
> Thorough the iron gates of life.

This is untranslatable: the meaning comes to us through the imagery or not at all; it can be "explained" and has been—it contains a highly complex intellectual concept—but the poetic meaning evaporates in the process; after all the explanations we must return to Marvell's image itself and allow the imagination to transmit the meaning to the intellect.

I will end with a quotation from Middleton Murry's essay on "Metaphor" in his *John Clare and Other Studies* (p. 91) of which you should read the whole.

> To the great poet his constant accumulation of vivid sense perceptions supplies the most potent means by which he articulates his spiritual intuitions, for recognitions of spiritual quality can be most forcefully and swiftly conveyed through analogous recognitions of sensuous quality.

So much for the "bodying forth" of the abstract in sensuous form. But what of all those images of which the literal element is already concrete? What of the two with which I illustrated the meaning of simile and metaphor, Burns's "O my luve is like a red, red rose", and Collins's

> Spring with dewy fingers cold
> Returns to deck their hallow'd mould.

Or, to continue Wordsworth's Sonnet to Milton,

> Thou hadst a voice whose sound is like the sea.

Or Keats's *Grecian Urn*,

> Thou still unravish'd bride of quietness.

Or Marvell's

> He hangs in shades the orange bright
> Like golden lamps in a green night.

Or, finally, the anonymous sixteenth-century lyric,

> Weep you no more, sad fountains,
>   What need you flow so fast? . . .
> But my sun's heavenly eyes
>   View not your weeping.

Why not in each case—the girl Burns loved,* Spring with its early morning flowers and dews, the sound of Milton's voice, the Urn, the oranges, the lover's weeping eyes and the beauty of his lady—give a direct description of their physical characteristics? They already appeal to the senses; if sensuousness is all, why superimpose upon them a second set of sensuous impressions? We have only to read the lines to know how much is gained, but what is it?

First, an immeasurable gain in *intensity*: the imagination receives the impact not of one sensuous impression, but of *two fused into one*. And the image not only thus doubles the impact, but in each case adds something to the literal object, again intensifying the impression. We see, at one and the same time, the still, pure whiteness of the urn and the virginal purity and radiance of the bride; the urn, still an urn, has taken on the bride's purity and virginity. Marvell's oranges remain oranges in the green shadows of the trees, but with their colour transformed

* An alternative interpretation is that it is not the girl but Burns's love for her which is "like a red, red rose"; the image in the context of the whole poem is ambiguous. The ambiguity, however, in no way invalidates the truth of the image; many of the greatest poetic images admit of more than one interpretation and this may be a major element in their greatness. In the deep levels of consciousness where imagery is born there is a complex of associations which defies logic; Burns has here, possibly without being aware of the richness and complexity of the associations upon which he was drawing, intuitively discovered an image which at one and the same time embodies the essence of the girl herself and of his "newly-sprung" love for her.

into the golden brightness of "lamps in a green night". Milton's voice has the deep resonance of the sea; the lover's tears are tears, but with the beauty of a clear crystalline mountain spring; his lady, while still a lady, has the radiance of the sun. And so with the rest.

But these images perform another function—and it is one which they share with all imagery: they are *selective*, and in their selectiveness make for economy of words (and thus again for intensity); the one sensuous impression, both by what it selects and by what it excludes, presents directly to our imagination what it might take many lines of descriptive verse to tell us. "Thou still unravish'd bride of quietness": at this point of the ode Keats did not want us to visualize the urn with all its attributes; the image of the "still unravish'd bride" has, in three words, selected the one impression which he needed and has, for the moment, rejected all the rest. So with Collins's Spring: the image has isolated the one aspect of Spring which the poet needed, the early morning freshness of the newly opened flowers, from all the other associations which the word calls up in our memories. And so with the "golden lamps in a green night". And so, equally, with "Death lays his icy hand on kings", the "fen of stagnant waters", and the rest. For this selectiveness is a quality of all imagery.

But if this—the "bodying forth" of the abstract, the doubling, or more than doubling, of the sensuous, and the economy, and hence concentration achieved by the image's selectiveness—were all, the intensity and depth of the impression which imagery makes upon the imagination would still be unexplained. We now return to Aristotle and Shelley. Here are the complete passages of which I quoted only the beginnings:

> But the greatest thing by far is to be a master of metaphor. It is the only thing which cannot be learnt from others, and it is also a sign of genius, *since a good metaphor implies an intuitive perception of the similarity of dissimilars.*

> Their [the poets'] language is vitally metaphorical, that is, *it marks the before unapprehended relationships of things.*

"An *intuitive* perception of the *similarity of dissimilars*", "*before unapprehended relationships*"—the two writers are saying the same thing: the poet's business is to penetrate, by imaginative intuition, below the surface of things to *a unity beneath their diversity*. Whether or not we theoretically accept the philosophical doctrine that there is unity behind diverse appearances, in poetic imagery we do in fact empirically discover it and experience it. What, to the eye of reason, could be more dissimilar than Burns's "luve" and a red, red rose? Had the girl's face been the colour of the rose it is doubtful whether Burns would have been attracted to her; she was certainly not the shape of a rose, and must have been supported by two legs and not attached to a bush by a single stem; it is unlikely that she smelt like a rose. What has happened is that the girl and the rose, utterly dissimilar in appearance, both had *a quality of beauty which struck the same chord* somewhere deep down in Burns's consciousness; they had, in fact, something in common, a "before unapprehended relationship", so that girl and rose produced in him the same imaginative response. Reason would have seen only the differences, but poetic intuition (which Aristotle says is a mark of genius) has discovered the affinity. Nothing, again, is to the physical eye more dissimilar than the sights and sounds of Spring and a Being placing flowers on a grave, nor even than a man shedding tears and a mountain stream, or than his lady and the sun; even the resonance of Milton's verse bears little physical resemblance to the sound of the sea. In each case the affinity lies not on the surface but somewhere in the unplumbed depths beyond the reach of reason. That is why imagery stirs us so profoundly; put the two objects side by side and each will make its own impact, one and one will be two; but let the poet by imaginative intuition see them as two manifestations of some one common principle, let him reveal to us their "before unapprehended relationship", and one and one may become not two but nearer to infinity.

Good and Bad Imagery

The maker of a good image is a *discoverer*, of a bad an *inventor*. A successful image is never the result of arbitrary choice; the affinity which it reveals was pre-existent, even though "before unapprehended". And the test—assuming that our imaginations are trained to respond to imagery—of whether an image is a discovery or an invention, is the degree to which the two elements become fused into one as we read the poem. In an "invented" image, even though grammatically it may be a metaphor and speak of one element as, and not as like, the other, the two objects obstinately refuse to unite; do what we may we continue to see (or, if the image is aural, hear) them as two separate entities; we may compare them and notice their resemblances, but that is all. Contrast with any of the images in the previous section (preferably re-reading them in their context in the poem) Wordsworth's poem *To a Daisy* (the one—he wrote two—beginning, "With little here to do or see"):

> A nun demure of lowly port,
> Or sprightly maiden of love's court,
> In thy simplicity the sport
>   Of all temptations;
> A queen in crown of rubies drest;
> A starveling in a scanty vest;
> Are all, as seems to suit thee best,
>   Thy appellations.

Try for yourself to *see* a daisy as, while remaining itself, having taken on anything of one or other of these figures, nun, maiden, queen, starveling; it is impossible; all one can do is to visualize daisy and nun, daisy and maiden, daisy and "queen in crown of rubies", daisy and starveling, placed side by side, and to think in what respects they are alike. There is no "before unapprehended relationship", no hidden "similarity" in what are superficially "dissimilar"; Wordsworth's conscious mind has placed two dissimilar objects in juxtaposition and asked us to notice certain real or supposed resemblances. And he himself knew this:

in his collected poems he classified the *Daisy* not under the heading of "Imagination" but of "Fancy". Here he is following Coleridge: "[The poet] diffuses a tone and spirit of unity, that blends, and (as it were) *fuses*, each into each, by *that synthetic power, to which I would exclusively appropriate the name of Imagination*" (*Biographia Literaria*, ch. XIV). And (*ibid.*, ch. XIII), of the imagination as the creative power: "*It dissolves, diffuses, dissipates, in order to re-create*"; that is to say, it breaks down the elements of the image into their component parts and reunites them into what is a new creation, something having the essentials of both but the inessentials of neither. But of the Fancy, which was what Wordsworth knew had been at work in the making of his *Daisy*, Coleridge goes on to say:

> FANCY, on the contrary, has no other counters to play with, but fixities and definites. The fancy is indeed no other than a mode of memory emancipated from the order of time and space; while it is blended with and modified by that empirical phenomenon of the will, which we express by the word Choice. But equally with the ordinary memory the Fancy must receive all its materials ready made from the law of association.

Wordsworth had consciously cast about in his memory for certain "ready made" "fixities and definites"; from them he *chose* the four which he has used, and rearranged them in time and space by setting them beside the daisy. Fusion, synthesis and re-creation have not taken place. An image should be a chemical compound; these are mechanical mixtures. And this because the two sides of each had no hidden affinity for the imagination to discover. Contrast these metaphors of Wordsworth's with those which he uses when his creative imagination is at work:

> . . . Hearing oftentimes
> The still sad music of humanity . . .

or

> Hence, *in a season of calm weather*,
> Though *inland* far we be,
> Our souls *have sight of that immortal sea*
> Which brought us hither,
> Can in a moment travel thither,
> And see the children *sport upon the shore*,
> *And hear the mighty waters rolling evermore.*

The Epic Simile

Up to this point, apart from briefly defining metaphor and simile on page 43, I have generally made no distinction between the two; I have chosen my examples of imagery indiscriminately from one or the other. This was intentional; until one has learnt to respond to an image as an image it only distracts the attention to stop and consider its grammatical form.

> England hath need of thee; she is a fen
> Of stagnant waters. . . .
>
> Thy soul was like a star and dwelt apart;
> Thou hadst a voice whose sound was like the sea. . . .

Does it matter, from the point of view of their impact upon the imagination, that the first of these images is formally a metaphor and the second and third are similes? Milton's soul has become as much a solitary star and his voice has as much taken on the sound of the sea as has England become a stagnant fen. In each the fusion is complete; the presence or absence of the word "like" is irrelevant *to our imaginative response*. The time comes when we need to study a poet's technique; then of course the distinction must be made. But to begin by sorting them out into their appropriate classes before we have learnt to recognize their common function is merely distracting.

But there is a class of simile which can be read only as simile and as nothing else: the epic or extended simile.* In all the similes I have so far quoted the image is so brief that, though in fact the two elements are separated by the word "like", the fusion of the two takes place almost instantaneously; we have reached the second element before we have had time clearly to visualize—or, in the case of an abstract word, form a mental concept of—the first as a separate entity. But in the epic simile each side, and especially the "metaphorical", may extend to many lines; the latter may depict a fully developed scene, or even tell a miniature short story; instantaneous fusion is impos-

* The epic simile was used by Homer, and as all later writers of epic took him as their model it has become a standard feature of the epic style.

sible; each of the two parts takes too long to read. Take, for example, Milton's Satan and Leviathan (*Paradise Lost*, I; lines 191–210):

> Thus Satan talking to his nearest Mate
> With head up-lift above the wave, and Eyes
> That sparkling blaz'd, his other Parts besides
> Prone on the Flood, extended long and large
> Lay floating many a rood, in bulk as huge
> As . . . that Sea-beast
> Leviathan, which God of all his works
> Created hugest that swim the Ocean stream;
> Him haply slumbring on the Norway foam
> The pilot of some small night-founder'd Skiff,
> Deeming some Island, oft, as Seamen tell,
> With fixed Anchor in his skaly rind
> Moors by his side under the Lee, while Night
> Invests the Sea, and wished Morn delayes:
> So stretcht out huge in length the Arch-fiend lay
> Chain'd on the burning Lake. . . .

Milton seems here simply to have juxtaposed the two separate and fully expanded pictures, Satan lying on the flood and the whale with the ship anchored to its side, and in the words "as", "so", asked us to compare them. But notice what in fact happens as we read. What Milton wants us to visualize is the immense size of Satan; he wants us not merely to *know* Satan's measurements ("many a rood"), but to *see* him as immeasurably bigger than any living thing that we have ever seen, or, unaided, have it in us to imagine. He begins with direct description: Satan, individualized in every part—*except* size; even if we know the extent of a rood we cannot picture it. Then the simile begins: "In bulk as huge as . . . that Sea-beast Leviathan, which God of all his works created hugest. . . ." Yes, "huge", "hugest"—but how huge? We are still left to supply the "hugeness" for ourselves. Now comes the "small night-founder'd Skiff", *something familiar whose size we can visualize, a yardstick by which to measure the rest.* Then, beside the Skiff is what *looks like an island*, "huge" enough to give it shelter and secure anchorage; the pilot moors the Skiff "under the Lee". Then, and not till then,

> *So* stretcht out huge in length the Arch-fiend lay . . .

and, far from comparing the two, we *transfer* the hugeness of the island-whale to Satan; Satan, while still himself, as we have visualized him "prone on the flood", has *taken on the whale's immensity*; the process has been delayed, but by the end the fusion is as complete as in a metaphor. And the delay has been essential for had Milton developed his simile less fully the whale's—and hence Satan's—size would still have remained unimaginable.

But notice that the only element of the picture which we have transferred to Satan is the whale's "hugeness"; when our eye returns to him all the rest, Skiff, pilot, the whole "story", is left behind. Vivid as was every detail, the simile only succeeds because all were perfectly subordinated to, and pointed towards, the one "before unapprehended relationship" between the traditional story which Milton has used and Satan. This is proof of Milton's genius; that you may appreciate the measure of his achievement—and the pitfalls which beset the less skilful maker of an epic simile—here is Matthew Arnold attempting to do the same thing—and failing; he is, ostensibly, trying to help us to visualize the tattooing on Sohrab's arm:

> Then, with weak hasty fingers, Sohrab loos'd
> His belt, and near the shoulder bar'd his arm,
> And show'd a sign in faint familiar points
> Prick'd: as a cunning workman, in Pekin,
> Pricks with vermilion some clear porcelain vase,
> An emperor's gift—at early morn he paints
> And all day long, and, when night comes, the lamp
> Lights up his studious forehead and thin hands:—
> So delicately prick'd the sign appear'd
> On Sohrab's arm. . . .
>
> (*Sohrab and Rustum*, lines 669–678.)

Here "transference" is quite impossible: Matthew Arnold's own eye has wandered from the essential "similarity", the design that was pricked, to the "pricker"; from first to last it is he, the "cunning workman", that we visualize and not his work; every detail, "in Pekin", "at early dawn", "the lamp", his "studious forehead and thin hands", points away from the one essential which we need to visualize, the painting on the vase. It is a nice little picture in itself, but that is all. Now return to Milton's Leviathan, or, for that matter, to any of his epic similes, and you will appreciate the difference.

Direct Description which fulfils the Function of Imagery

The proposition upon which all the foregoing has been based is that because poetry, to appeal to the imagination, must be sensuous, therefore the poet must use imagery. And this is true: Aristotle was right when he said that it is in his intuitions of the "similarity of dissimilars" that the poet shows his genius. But this is not to say that direct sensuous description plays no part in poetry: nothing could add to the sensuous impact or poetic appeal of Milton's Paradise in Book IV of *Paradise Lost*, or of the table set with fruits and sweets in *The Eve of St. Agnes*. Where, as in each of these, it is the sensuous richness of the thing in itself to which the poet wants our imagination to respond—where there is no inner significance to reveal—imagery can be dispensed with. Both of these passages of description are setting the scene for something else—for the narrative in which the "meaning" of the poem lies. Both, it is true, reinforce this "meaning": the incomparable beauty and richness of Eden are the measure of God's creative power and of the lavishness of His generosity to the human race for whom it was created; throughout *The Eve of St. Agnes* every descriptive passage contributes to the "atmosphere" of passionate romantic young love which is the poem's theme. But each description is description and nothing more; by no stretching of the meaning of the word could it be classed as "imagery".

But elsewhere in poetry we do find instances of description direct in itself—literal, not metaphorical; descriptions of some actual scene or object which is, perhaps, the ostensible subject of the poem—which serve a different function: though direct in their form, what they say to the imagination is akin to metaphor; they are not only themselves, *they stand for something else*, and, where such descriptions and metaphor and simile are intermixed, we may pass from one to the other without being aware of the transition. They are not imagery—the word has a technical meaning which we cannot change—but they fulfil its purpose. As much as true imagery they are "bodyings-forth"; if we read them as straight description and nothing more we miss the meaning of the poem. Thus Keats's *Ode to Autumn*: the—literal—vines, apples, hazel nuts, gourds, and the "small gnats" and "full grown lambs" are as much embodyings of Keats's meaning as are the "close bosom-friend of the maturing sun" or as the personification of autumn "sitting careless on the granary floor" or "fast asleep / Drows'd with the fume of poppies". For Keats's "moment of imaginative experience" had been of something far deeper that of the sensuous beauty of the scene in itself; what he has seen is the significance of Autumn, the season of, at one and the same time, the climax of the richness of fruition and fulfilment, and yet as the melancholy end. And everything in the poem, whether literal or metaphorical, is there to tell us this. So with the *Grecian Urn*—it is the urn itself, with its (literal) scenes of lovers and of the priest coming to the sacrifice, which embodies the meaning: the whole ode is, in effect, an extended image; the formal metaphors are images within an image.

Keats's odes are highly complex. I will end with a poem so deceptively simple that its very simplicity may, if we read it at its face value, obscure the profundity and universality of what it has to say to us. It was, in fact, this poem which first led me to question the validity of the hard and fast distinction between direct description and imagery.* It is Hardy's *In the Time of "The Breaking of the Nations"*:

* And, I should add, the answer to my questioning was suggested to me by Cecil Day Lewis's *The Poetic Image*. But, because I was primarily concerned to find an answer to my own question, my application of his principle diverges widely, though I hope legitimately, from his. For his interpretation read his chapter, "The Pattern of Images".

Only a man harrowing clods
    In a slow silent walk
With an old horse that stumbles and nods,
    Half asleep as they stalk.

Only thin smoke without flame
    From the heaps of couch-grass;
Yet this will go onward the same
    Though Dynasties pass.

Yonder a maid and her wight
    Come whispering by;
War's annals will cloud into night
    Ere their story die.

What Hardy here seems to be saying is, in the first two stanzas, that—literally—a particular method of primitive farming will continue to be practised whatever kings may come and go, and, in the third, that wars will be forgotten sooner than a pair of young lovers. In fact, of course, even at a first and superficial reading, this is not the impression that one gains; just because of the pictorial quality of the poem, and allowing for a certain amount of poetic licence in "will go onward the same", one, I think, rather responds directly to the nostalgic attraction of a slow-moving, stable, traditional, "natural" way of life in contrast to the flashiness of "Dynasties", and to the beauty of young love as compared with war, without even considering the literal truth of the assertion. But if this is our response it is very far from Hardy's intention: what is embodied, though not overtly expressed, in the poem is hard fact, a scientific truth which, put baldly, amounts to this: the survival of the human race depends, not upon what king happens to be on the throne or on victory or defeat in any given war, but upon agriculture and mating; these not only will, but must, endure if man is to survive. Each scene thus stands for more than itself; it is only when the imagination sees through its particularity to the universal which it typifies that Hardy's meaning can be apprehended; each visual picture is, though the method is different, as much a "bodying forth" as is Shirley's "Death lays his icy hand on kings". What I think must have happened was that Hardy already had, lying dormant in his mind as a theoretical concept, the truth that only by food-production and the reproduction of its kind can humanity survive; then one day during the First World War (the poem was written in 1917), when victory seemed to be the most important thing in the world, he saw this familiar every-day scene; his "moment of imaginative experience" came to him, the general became embodied in the particular, and he knew that *these*—the fight to keep back the jungle (the burning couch-grass), the primitive scratching of the soil for food, and boy and girl falling in love—were the permanent things compared with which victory or defeat in any one war at a particular point of time was of no enduring consequence. Thus his pictures, without being formally metaphors, fulfil their function: they embody a universal truth in sensuous form, and by so doing bring it home to our imaginations as no general statement could. They are not imagery, but they work as if they were.

CHAPTER IV

TRAGEDY

The Catharsis of Pity and Fear

Any discussion of tragedy must start from Aristotle. For not only was he, as far as we know, the first to attempt to define the tragic experience, but his definition of tragedy and analysis of the effect which it has on our emotions has been so assimilated into critical thought and language that, if we are unfamiliar with his words "the catharsis of pity and fear" in their context, and with the probable meaning which, from a study of his other works, scholars believe he intended, much of what we read will be either unintelligible to us or, worse, misleading. But not only so: the definition itself, even though it may not go all the way, comes nearer to getting to the root of the problem than any other which has been attempted.

For tragedy does present a problem. We go to the theatre not as a painful duty or penance, but for pleasure; why, then, do we choose *for pleasure* to witness the representation upon the stage of the most extreme, agonizing, heart-breaking suffering which, were it to happen in actuality, we would shrink, not only from witnessing, but even from imagining? And further—and this is the paradox—why is it that it is not the callous, the brutalized, the insensitive, but, in general, the very people who are most sensitive to the suffering of others—the imaginative and the compassionate—who make up the audience when great tragedy is performed? What is it that the tragic dramatist has done to his raw material to turn that which would cause us unmixed pain in real life into a profoundly satisfying and pleasure-giving spiritual experience? Why, to give a concrete example, would we go a hundred miles to avoid seeing a negro soldier murder his white wife and commit suicide, and yet we will travel many hundreds of miles for the pleasure of seeing a performance of *Othello* upon the stage?

Not—and this cannot be too much stressed—because the dramatist has dressed up his horrifying material in pretty language. The language of poetic tragedy is, it is true, often of great beauty, and this does account for a part of our pleasure. But the language is there for one purpose, and one alone: to transmit to us the content of the play—not to stand between us and the theme but to carry it home to our emotions and our imagination with the utmost possible truth and intensity. And if, as in great tragedy it does, it fulfils this function, then it must be the content itself which, despite the pain, gives us an "overbalance of pleasure"; it must be the suffering itself which has in some way been transformed from what we would be aware of in "real life".

So to Aristotle's definition: "A tragedy, then, is the imitation of an action that is serious and also, as having magnitude, complete in itself; . . . in a dramatic, not in a narrative form; *with incidents arousing pity and fear, wherewith to accomplish its catharsis of such emotions*" (Aristotle's *The Art of Poetry*, Bywater's translation, p. 35) and (*ibid.*, p. 50): "Pity is occasioned by undeserved misfortune, and fear by that of one like ourselves." And the first thing to notice here is the emotions which Aristotle tells us that tragedy rouses in us: not horror, disgust, physical revulsion, as do scenes of violence in real life, but *pity* and *fear*, pity for undeserved suffering,* and fear because, the sufferer being "one like ourselves", we know that such suffering is possible for ourselves; we are all in it together. So far so good: instead of arousing horror, a degrading and brutalizing emotion, tragedy, by directing our attention to the undeservedness of the suffering, replaces it by pity, by compassion, one of the purest of human emotions, and at the same time it forces us to face the truth that "no man

* For the extent to which the sufferings of the hero are undeserved, see Chapter VIII, "Notes on Aristotle's Poetics", pp. 153–6.

is an island", that we ourselves, in virtue of the common humanity we share with the hero, are not immune. A very salutary lesson. Clearly, therefore, tragedy is "a good thing", morally good for us, as are many other painful experiences.

But if this is all, where is the pleasure? To witness a tragedy might indeed be a moral duty, but one to be not enjoyed but endured. But it is not all: Aristotle goes on: "wherewith to accomplish its catharsis of such emotions". It is not the arousing of the emotions in itself which is at the heart of the tragic experience, but *something which happens to them* when they are aroused. And this "something" is indicated by the (untranslated) Greek word, *catharsis*.

The problem then is: what did Aristotle mean by catharsis? And here I am following Humphry House's interpretation of the word in his *Aristotle on the Art of Poetry*. All scholars (with only rare exceptions) have been agreed upon the main principle: that the word is a term drawn from Greek medicine, and that Aristotle's meaning is that the pleasure we experience in tragedy is due to the fact that it acts as a psychological medicine, restoring us to emotional health; that our pity and fear as we habitually experience them are, in some sense, unhealthy, and hence painful; that the business of tragedy is, in some way, to remove their morbidity, and that the removal of this morbidity causes pleasure to outweigh pain; when we enter the theatre we are emotionally sick, when we leave it we are well. The trouble, however, has been to discover the nature of the illness and how the medicine works. The usual translation of "catharsis" has been "purging", and it is true that the Greeks, including Aristotle himself, often use the word in this sense: a cathartic is an evacuant which rids the body of some unwanted matter, specifically, in Greek medicine, of a superfluity of one of the "humours". In its crudest interpretation this has been taken to mean that when we see a tragedy we expend our whole store of pity and fear upon the imaginary sufferings of the hero, and that the resultant pleasure lies in our having emptied ourselves of these painful emotions. But this hardly needs refuting, for were we to leave the theatre pitiless and having forgotten that we ourselves must be prepared to face suffering we would be morally not in better but in far worse health than when we entered it, and, in any case, all of us who have ever been moved by great tragedy know perfectly well that, far from being emptied of pity and of the awareness of suffering as part of the human lot, our sense of both has been immeasurably deepened by the experience. Far more acceptable interpretations are those of Butcher (*Aristotle's Theory of Poetry and the Fine Arts*) and Bywater (in his commentary on his translation of Aristotle's *Poetics*). But both still assume the translation "purging". Humphry House's innovation lies in his proof that for Aristotle the word catharsis had another meaning—that of balancing and bringing into due proportion. And this seems to meet the case. His argument is so technical and closely reasoned that any summary must be inadequate; it is essential to read the book itself. But, briefly: by comparing Aristotle's use of the word catharsis in the *Poetics* with his use of it in his other works, and also by going to his analysis of the emotions, including pity and fear, especially in the *Nichomachean Ethics*, he has found that, although Aristotle does frequently use the word in the sense of an evacuant, "it is also used for a *qualitative* change in the body, in the restoration of a proper equilibrium (e.g. between heat and cold); and a state of health depends upon the maintenance of this proper equilibrium" (p. 106). In other words, catharsis in this sense does not rid the body of any element, but restores it to health by bringing the elements into balance so that each may function as it should. Having then marshalled his evidence for this use of the word and for its application to emotional as well as to physical disorders, he finally goes to the *Nichomachean Ethics* for Aristotle's statement of what constitutes emotional (and hence moral) health; the passage ends:

> . . . both *fear* . . . and *pity* and in general pleasure and pain may be felt both too much and too little, and in both cases not well; but to feel them *at the right times, with reference to the right objects, towards the right people, with the right motive, and in the right way,* is what is intermediate and best, and this is the characteristic of virtue [Italics mine].

Returning from ethics to tragedy, House concludes:

> A tragedy rouses the emotions from potentiality to actuality by worthy and adequate stimuli; it controls them by directing them to the right objects in the right way; and exercises them, within the limits of the play, as the emotions of the good man would be exercised . . . this is what Aristotle calls κάθαρσις [*catharsis*] [pp. 109, 110].

And this, in fact, is what, I think, most of us would agree is the effect upon us of a great tragedy.

What does the Tragic Dramatist do to his Raw Material so that his Play may produce the Catharsis of Pity and Fear?

The question with which we began can now be restated: in what way does the tragic dramatist treat his pain- and horror-producing material—the incidents as they would appear to us in actuality—so as to arouse our emotions by worthy and adequate stimuli, to control them, and to direct them to the right objects in the right way—and thus to produce, not horror and unmitigated pain, but the catharsis of pity and fear? The catharsis of pity and fear is his end, but what (given his inborn genius, without which he can do nothing) are the means by which he attains it? What is it that he, in each case, has done to his material which explains the difference between the last act of *Othello* and what we would be aware of were a negro soldier to murder his wife and commit suicide before our eyes? Or between the third Act of *King Lear* and what we would see and hear were we in fact to meet a poor old madman wandering in a storm? Or between the final scene of the *Oedipus Tyrannus* and the same happenings as they would have appeared to us had we ourselves been present?

And because in each case it is the "real-life" scene which would have stimulated what are clearly the wrong, the untragic, emotions, one point is self-evident:

Great Tragedy can never be Realistic

For, by definition, a realistic play is one which sets out to give us the impression: This is a photographically accurate representation of the "real thing"; it aims to create the illusion: this is what, had we been present, we should have seen and heard. And, as we have already seen, what in the tragic story we should have seen and heard would have caused us only pain and horror. The resultant play would be, not tragedy, but a horror-play or Grand Guignol,* something which would appeal to the same morbid fascination with cruelty which, in the past, drew crowds to witness the public hangings at Tyburn, or today is pandered to by the less reputable Sunday papers.

And this is because, while we should have seen *what* happened, we could know little or nothing of *why*. We should see the violence, the bloodshed, the outer manifestations of suffering; we might hear cries or curses or incoherent words. But of the *mental* agony, of the tormented passions, of the good and evil at war in the souls of the actors, we could know nothing. For human beings are inarticulate. And this even in their calmest moments; none of us can, at any time, communicate what is deepest in ourselves. We may talk endlessly, and possibly with the greatest precision, of our opinions, our experiences or up to a point of our feelings; but always there comes the time where communication becomes impossible; we may say, "I am so miserable I wish I were dead", "I love him beyond words" (notice "beyond words"), or "I am so happy I feel as if I were in heaven", but the nature of the misery, the love, the happiness—what it feels like to be miserable, in love, or blissfully happy—we not only cannot communicate to others, *we cannot even find words to formulate to ourselves*. The most we can hope for is that some sympathetic friend may, by intuition, appreciate something of what we cannot say. And this even when we have leisure to collect our thoughts and search for words; in moments of crisis, of mental turmoil, of physical fear, of violent action, we are

* So called from the theatre in Paris at which such plays were produced.

probably capable of no more than an exclamation, a cry, a gesture—or perhaps some bathetic triviality. And in a realistic play, if it is to carry conviction, the characters must be only a little more articulate than this.

But the whole business of the writer of tragedy—the means by which he turns physical horror into the catharsis of pity and fear—is to reveal the "why". The theme of tragedy is not—although the "action" is essential*—the series of happenings which culminate in the downfall and (probably) the death of the hero, but this very inner conflict and mental suffering, the war of the passions, of good and evil in the hero's soul, which in a realistic representation must remain a blank. If the writer of tragedy does not break with the whole convention of realism and give to his characters a command of words and a power of self-expression which, if the play in other respects purported to be a "slice of life", would be utterly incredible, the whole tragic theme—the inner conflict and the mental sufferings which actuate and are actuated by the "happenings"—must remain unexpressed. Imagine a realistically inarticulate Macbeth: without his (unnatural) gift of poetic utterance the play would be little more than a blood bath, a "shocker", Grand Guignol; were Othello unable to express the torment in his soul we should see nothing in his conduct but revolting and sadistic cruelty; Lear, a poor crazy old man wandering in a storm, would, had Shakespeare not given him his own command of words to reveal the volcanic storm within him, be a shocking sight and no more. And imagine a Phèdre deprived of an eloquence which is Racine's and not her own. And so with Greek drama, the *Oedipus Tyrannus*, the *Agamemnon*, the *Electra*. In each, and in every play which produces the true tragic impact, were the characters to speak naturalistically we should be aware of nothing but the horrible appearances; the passions, the mental agony, the moral struggles, the inner imaginings, the confrontation in the soul of the hero of good and evil—all that moves us to the very depths of our beings in the plays as they are—would

* Cf. Chapter VIII, "Notes on Aristotle's Poetics", pp. 150–2.

be missing. In every true tragedy it is by the unnaturalistic gift of words with which the dramatist has endowed his characters that the tragic theme is expressed.

And from this it follows that:

All Great Tragedy is written in Verse

Of course, the vast majority of "unhappy" plays, of plays in which the characters suffer and perhaps die, are, today at least, written in prose. And in many of these plays the dramatist does, despite the apparent naturalism of the speech, give to his characters a gift for self-expression far beyond that which they could in actuality possess, and thus he enables them to reveal their mental processes and inner life as no "real" people could. In other respects they are behaving and speaking so "naturally" that we do not notice that their speech is not quite their own but their creator's. But still the fact remains that they must continue to sound "natural"—their speech must go little beyond the common idiom of their class and situation and their self-revelation must remain within the bounds of credibility, or the whole illusion will be shattered. Such plays may have profound psychological insight, they may move us, but none of them has the impact of tragedy; none penetrate to those deepest levels of our being where, and where alone, the catharsis of pity and fear can be achieved. Compare for yourselves, if you are familiar with the two plays, the state of mind in which you leave the theatre after a production of *Hedda Gabler* and of *King Lear*. And this difference is not only due to Shakespeare's greater genius; he and Ibsen have set out to write two different kinds of play, the one tragedy, the other something else, a "something" for which prose is the natural vehicle. And the difference between the two kinds is primarily one of *magnitude*—of the degree to which the characters are built on the grand scale, big enough to embrace in themselves the heights and depths of human experience, and to fill us, not only with pity for someone like ourselves, but with awe for someone incomparably greater. Hedda is a *little* character; it is, in fact, her pettiness which is her undoing; whole ranges of human passion are utterly beyond her; she has not got it in her even to conceive of them. She suffers, yes—to the limits of her ability. But how limited she is! She cannot move us to the depths of our being, for she has not such depths in herself. The pain of the play—and it is painful—is mitigated not by the catharsis of pity and fear, but by our intellectual interest in her character and our profound appreciation of Ibsen's psychological insight. It is a great play of its kind, but it has nothing in common with tragedy. And even in Ibsen's *The Wild Duck*, although it is a more moving play than *Hedda Gabler* and arouses profound *pity*, the final effect is not the catharsis of pity and fear but pain, for here again the characters are built on too small a scale to transcend their sufferings and to sum up the sublime heights and abysmal depths of which humanity is capable. And this is just what *King Lear* does: he is titanic—human, yet larger than life—not one little old man but humanity itself, with all its strength and weakneses, at the end of its tether. He is an archetypal figure who fills us not only with pity but with awe. And although it is true that Lear is unique in his stature, not one of Shakespeare's other heroes, nor the hero of any other great tragedy, is an "average man"; all tower above common humanity; for all their faults and weakness, they are giants among pigmies. And this in their virtues as well as in their capacity for suffering. For the theme of tragedy is not evil alone, but the conflict of *good* and evil, and the good must be on as transcendent a scale as is the evil. Tragedy must indeed show us the worst, but the worst redeemed by a vision of the beauty of goodness. The evil may, it is true, at least on the physical plane, have overcome the good—hence our pity and fear. But yet the beauty remains—beauty as much beyond our common experience as is the evil—and neither suffering nor death can destroy it. This is why the final impression left by a great tragedy remains one of moral invigoration rather than of depression or despair. The world is indeed worse than we had imagined it, *but it is also better*. It holds, it is true, a Goneril, a Regan, an Iago—but it also holds a Cordelia, a Desdemona, and, the evil in him purged by suffering, a redeemed Lear made up of love and humility, and an Othello whose heart is broken *because*, once rid of the poison which Iago has injected into him, it is his own nobility which reveals to him the full horror of what he has done; even with Macbeth, the Shakespearian hero who sinks deepest in evil, it is because he has potentialities of goodness so much above the average that his downfall is tragic, and this is how, at the end, he himself sees his own tragedy.

And every one of these plays is written, at least in the scenes of tragic tension, in verse.

And so to sum up: the business of tragedy is not with the average, the familiar, the everyday, it is with ultimates, ultimate heights, ultimate depths, the best and worst in human nature. Its scale must be sublime. And, although prose is an adequate medium for a *Hedda Gabler*, every play which passes the test of tragedy is, in fact, written in verse.

Why Verse?

Very briefly, the reason why verse is the medium of tragedy is, first and foremost, that the theme of tragedy—the heights and depths, the passions, the conflict of good and evil and the ultimate of mental suffering which lie behind appearances—can only be apprehended by the poetic imagination; every reason for which any other poet uses verse holds good equally for the tragic dramatist. But even were it possible for the tragic theme to be expressed in prose, still verse would have its function: its use ensures absolutely that what we see before us on the stage can never by the remotest possibility be mistaken for a representation of "the real thing", and thus prepares us to accept without incredulity a power of self-expression which in "real life", or in a play purporting to represent it, would be impossible. From the very moment the characters begin to speak in Greek iambics, in Alexandrines or in iambic pentameters, we know absolutely, even if we do not consciously formulate the knowledge to ourselves, that *this is art and not nature*, that what we are witnessing is not intended to be a representation of actuality, but a dramatic poet's re-creation of actuality in terms which will reveal its inner meaning. At one stroke all expectation of realism has been eliminated: the actors are speaking *as* they would not (and could not) and thus we feel no incongruity when they go on to say *what* they could not. And once all expectation of realism is thus eliminated the poet is free to lend to his characters all the resources of his own art and genius, his own gift for words and his own command of imagery—to make them, in fact, poets able to speak directly to the poetic imagination of the audience.

Dramatic Poetry

This, however, is not to say that every time a character in poetic drama opens his lips he must burst into "poetry" in the conventional sense of the word. In classical and still more in neo-classical tragedy with its rigid adherence to the rules of idealization and generalization,* it is true that the style tends to be "elevated"; Racine, for all his restrained passion, allows little individuality to his characters' diction; all equally speak Racinian Alexandrines composed, in accordance with the neo-classical rule, of words chosen for their "elevation" above familiar colloquial speech; although the passion is their own its expression is undisguisedly Racine's. Yet even here the style is not that which Racine would have used had he been writing a poem in his own person; it is specifically a *dramatic* style, one evolved for one purpose and for one purpose only, to be spoken by characters caught up in a dramatic situation.

For dramatic poetry differs from lyrical just in this: it is not "poetry for poetry's sake" but the poetic expression of "action" in the broadest sense of the word. The dramatic poet's business is not to write a series of "poems" for his characters to speak, however beautiful these poems may be, but to give to them poetic words by which, in the stress of action, they may express themselves. The words, of course, and their metrical arrangement, are

* See Chapter VI, "Classical and Romantic", pp. 107–8.

the poet's and not their own, but always, if the poetry is to be dramatic, they must come from within outwards—within, that is to say, *that character* as he is *in that moment of time*; the character has, indeed, been given a miraculous power of self-expression, but always the words and metre are there to transmit to our imagination what he would, in that situation, have expressed had he had such a power. The poetry arises out of the impact between character and situation as a spark arises when flint strikes steel, and, like the spark, its function is light, illumination. And if this illumination comes, whether the words in themselves are "beautiful" or "ugly" is irrelevant; their poetry lies in their power to bring alive in our imagination with the utmost intensity and precision the inner, the psychological, the emotional, drama.

And this is Shakespeare's supreme greatness as a writer of dramatic poetry. Abandoning all rule as to what is "poetical" and what is not, and drawing upon the whole range of the English language in his day, from its most exotically "poetical" to its most down-to-earth and colloquial, he gives to each character not only the words but the metrical rhythm in which he can most dramatically express *himself*. In the late mature tragedies, that is to say: if you want to learn the difference between "poetry for poetry's sake" and poetry as dramatic expression, compare the lyricism of his one* early tragedy, *Romeo and Juliet*, with any of the late tragedies. In *Romeo and Juliet* alone among his tragedies does he write "poems" in his own non-dramatic poetical style for his characters to speak—*set-pieces*, beautiful in themselves but clearly Shakespeare's and not their own. We do not often notice the incongruity, for the play itself is of the nature of a love-lyric; the lovers are little more than a poet's dream of ideal romantic passion, which even the presence of the nurse does not bring down to earth. So we accept that Juliet, when waiting for Romeo, should in her "Gallop apace, ye fiery footed steeds / Towards Phoebus' lodging. . ." express herself in what is, in fact, an adaptation of an Italian "evening ode"; it does not occur to us that both the construction and the

* *Titus Andronicus* is not a tragedy; it is a horror-play.

imagery are those of a professional poet and not of a girl of fourteen; it is all a part of the spirit of the play. But when even the otherwise earthy and colloquial Old Capulet, Lady Capulet or Mercutio break into Shakespearian lyricism or conceits it is clear that characterization and dramatic fitness have been cast to the winds; the poetry is not an integral part of the play; it is an added decoration—the work of a young lyrical poet in love with his own art. The play is, in fact, as Granville-Barker has called it, a lyrical tragedy, lyrical both in its treatment of love and in its often non-dramatic poetic style.

But when Shakespeare came to write the late, great, tragedies his whole technique had changed. Poetry not only as lovely as, but far more lovely than, the lyricism of *Romeo and Juliet* remains —lines of incantatory melody, of sensuous imagery, magically haunting in their beauty: Macbeth's "Sleep that knits up the ravell'd sleave of care, / The death of each day's life, sore nature's bath . . ."; in *Antony and Cleopatra*, Iras' "Finish, good lady; the bright day is done / And we are for the dark", and Cleopatra's "Peace, peace! / Dost thou not see my baby at my breast / That sucks the nurse asleep" and Hamlet's "Absent thee from felicity awhile"—and innumerable others. But not one of these is a "set-piece" which can be isolated from its dramatic context and treated as "a poem in itself", irrespective of who spoke it and when; each, like the spark from flint on steel, arises out of and exists only to irradiate with the light of beauty the one moment of time, the meeting of character and circumstance, to which it belongs; each speaks with the voice, not of Shakespeare speaking in his own person, but of the one individual for whom he has created it; and none is decorative; each is integral to the play. And all are "beautiful" only because at that point beauty was essential to Shakespeare's dramatic purpose. But as dramatic poetry—that is to say, as words which bring the situation home to the imagination with maximum power—they are no more poetical than are Lear's "Rumble thy bellyful! Spit, fire! Spout rain", or than Hamlet's "Who would fardels bear / To grunt and sweat under a weary life", in both of which not only the words themselves, but the harsh and unmelodious movement of the lines is an essential part of the dramatic expressiveness. And perhaps nowhere is the "flint on steel" principle more perfectly exemplified than in Macbeth's recognition of what he has made of his own life:

> Out, out, brief candle.
> Life's but a walking shadow; a poor player,
> That struts and frets his hour upon the stage,
> And then is heard no more; it is a tale
> Told by an idiot, full of sound and fury,
> Signifying nothing.

No one in the world but Shakespeare could have written this, but it is Macbeth who is speaking; the words, given to him, it is true, by Shakespeare, are his own.*

The convention within which Shakespeare wrote, and which he shared with his English contemporaries is, of course, far freer than that of classical drama. Racine and the neo-classicists apart, even in Greek drama there was a degree of formality which would have forbidden Shakespeare's most daring experiments with language. Nevertheless, always in poetic drama the poetry must arise out of, and be the expression of, the dramatic situation; it should never be an added decoration, poetry for poetry's sake.

Imagery in Tragedy

The tragic dramatist, of course, uses imagery as does every other poet—without it his plays would not be poetry; it is one of the essentials of his art, and if no other justification for the use of verse existed, this alone, that only in verse are we prepared to accept poetic images which the naturalism of prose would render totally incongruous, would make the use of verse essential. But besides the function which it fulfils in all poetry imagery has in

* Not, of course, of the historical Macbeth—he would never have seen a player "strutting and fretting his hour upon the stage"—but of the anachronistic Macbeth of Shakespeare's imagination.

tragedy a very special use; it is one of the means by which the tragic dramatist solves one of his major problems: that of ensuring that the scenes of violence and bloodshed which, whether enacted upon the stage or, in classical tragedy, narrated (and narrated violence can be horrible), are an ingredient of every tragedy, may produce not physical revulsion and nausea but the catharsis of pity and fear. For imagery can be used *to interpose another picture* between our eye and the bloodshed and horror, or sheer nastiness, of the physical action. And not only *an* other picture, but another picture which embodies in itself the inner drama which it is the tragic dramatist's business to transmit to us. Take Othello's last speech; at the end he is going to stab himself, a revolting sight to see. This is what Shakespeare does:

> . . . I pray you, in your letters,
> When you shall these unlucky deeds relate,
> Speak of me as I am; nothing extenuate,
> Nor set down aught in malice: then must you speak
> Of one that loved not wisely but too well;
> Of one not easily jealous, but, being wrought,
> Perplex'd in the extreme; *of one whose hand,*
> *Like the base Indian, threw a pearl away*
> *Richer than all his tribe;* of one whose subdued eyes,
> Albeit unused to the melting mood,
> *Drop tears as fast as the Arabian trees*
> *Their medicinable gum.* Set you down this;
> And say besides, that in Aleppo once,
> Where a malignant and a turban'd Turk
> Beat a Venetian and traduc'd the state.
> I took by the throat the circumcised dog,
> And smote him—thus.

And with the word "thus", *before we have had time to focus our eyes upon the figure standing before us upon the stage*, the deed is done. The effect is not, of course, achieved solely by imagery; there is, first, Othello's direct statement of the moral nature of his tragedy, of his "error of judgement", and, finally, the "turban'd Turk"; it is not from an image but from a literal scene in Aleppo, a picture of the unfallen Othello in his former greatness and nobility, that our eye is ultimately recalled by the word "thus". Nevertheless it is the two images which not only, by their sensuous loveliness, irradiate the whole scene with beauty, and by their setting, India and Arabia, are most remote from the scene before us, but which "body forth" to our imagination Othello's true tragedy: the first, Desdemona an "orient pearl" thrown away in ignorance, the second, Othello's tears of mental agony and remorse turned to "medicinable gum". And it is these two images which remain in our memory and transmute Othello's death into a thing of tragic beauty.

Compare this with the one and only scene in Shakespeare's tragedies (as distinct from *Titus Andronicus*, the "horror-play") which by general consent is so physically revolting as to be intolerable upon the stage, the blinding of Gloucester in *King Lear*. The incident in itself is probably no worse than others which we accept: the difference lies in Shakespeare's method. For here the words, far from giving us something else to look at, or to think about, *themselves describe the physical act*—in fact, accentuate its horror, for they bring visually before us more than an audience could see: "Out, vile jelly!" Shakespeare may have had good reason for writing as he has: he may have known that nothing short of sheer physical nausea could bring home to his audience the utter barbarity of Regan's cruelty; it may be, too, that we are too squeamish to face what a Tudor audience could take in its stride. Yet the fact remains that the scene stands alone, and had Shakespeare used this method habitually his tragedies would be "horror-plays". And imagery is one, though far from the only, means by which he lifts the action from the physical to the moral and spiritual plane, and thus, in Humphry House's words, "rouses the emotions from potentiality to actuality by worthy and adequate stimuli" and "controls them by directing them to the right objects in the right way".

Conclusion

So, to sum up. We began with the question: what does the tragic dramatist do to his raw material so as to transmute it into tragedy? Rejecting realism, he must re-create it so as to reveal not appearances only but their causes—the inner drama of the passions and the moral conflict between the forces of good and evil and the mental sufferings of the hero. And this inner drama can only be apprehended by the poetic imagination; the tragic dramatist must use all the resources of the poet's art; thus he must write in verse, for only so can he both remove all expectation of photographic representation, and transmit to our imagination, by the rhythm of the verse itself and by the use of poetic imagery, the tragic content of the play and so produce in us, not unmitigated pain, but the "catharsis of pity and fear".

Note 1. Shakespeare's Use of Prose

You will have noticed that throughout this chapter I have spoken as if the tragic dramatist must write exclusively in verse, and in classical tragedy of course he does. But for the sake of simplicity and in order to avoid confusing the issue I have ignored Shakespeare's frequent use of prose. Here two problems must be kept distinct: that of the use of verse (and the poetic imagery which goes with it) to transmit the poetic content of the play to the imagination, and the secondary one of its use to eliminate all expectation of realism. As to the first, Shakespeare in general (though there are exceptions to the rule) uses prose in scenes of relatively relaxed dramatic and emotional tension or for rustic or ignorant characters (the Porter in *Macbeth*, for instance, or the Grave-diggers in *Hamlet*) who stand outside the action and unwittingly provide an ironical commentary upon the doings of their betters. And such relaxed scenes are essential, for without them we should be strained to breaking point, battered until we ceased to respond; in classical tragedy (and often in Shakespeare) they may be written in a more relaxed verse or, in Greek tragedy, take the form of Choric Odes, but alternatively a drop into prose can serve the purpose. And then, as the emotional and poetic tension increases the verse rhythm takes over. But Shakespeare does occasionally use prose in his scenes of highest tension, notably for the sleep-walking Lady Macbeth, and the prose here has as highly charged a poetic impact as any verse could have. But it is not, as are the majority of Shakespeare's prose interludes, the colloquial prose of every-day speech; it is poetic prose, with a hallucinatory musical rhythm which, while by its lack of the ordered recurrence of verse it reflects, dramatically, Lady Macbeth's broken and disordered mind, yet has the unnaturalistic musical quality which permits of "all the perfumes of Arabia", a phrase which in naturalistic speech would be impossible. This scene, however, is exceptional, and had it not been for his mastery of every modulation of speech Shakespeare could not have given it its poetic impact. And as a general rule it is true to say that he uses prose to relax tension, verse to heighten it.

As to the question of realism: the early *Romeo and Juliet* apart, the problem only arises in *King Lear* and *Coriolanus*; all the other late tragedies open with verse and so tell us what to expect. But I think the answer is a simple one: it is a matter of the audience's familiarity with the convention of poetic drama. The audience at the Globe knew perfectly well that they had come to see a verse play, for they knew no other kind of drama; they arrived in the "verse" frame of mind, and a few lines of prose were accepted for what they were, a preliminary before the expected irrealism of the iambic pentameters began. So with us today: we know that we have come to see poetic tragedy and hardly even notice that the play opens with naturalistic prose.

Note 2. "The Double Level of Consciousness"

This phrase, "the double level of consciousness", I have borrowed from J. B. Priestley, who used it in one of a series of broadcasts on Network Three to describe the state of mind in which we watch a play. It is to him that I am indebted, not only for the phrase itself, but, except for the application of the principle to poetic drama, for much of what follows, and, too, for the clarification in my own mind of what I had already, of course, been aware of but had never clearly formulated. The point is this: when we get to the theatre, however realistic the play may be, we never for one moment mistake it for the real thing; always, from first to last, we know that we are sitting in, it may be, the stalls or, it may be, the gallery, that we have come to see a play, that the stage is a stage, that the actors are actors who have learnt their parts by heart, and that the man or woman whom, perhaps, we see lying dead before us will very soon appear alive and well, bowing and smiling before the curtain. And yet, at one and the same time, upon the second level of consciousness, we are, if the play is a good one and well acted, in imagination completely emotionally involved, and "believe every word" of it. Simultaneously we, watching Dame Peggy Ashcroft acting the part of Hedda Gabler, are on the alert to see exactly how *she* interprets the part, *appraise her as an actress*, and yet never for a moment cease to believe in Hedda herself. The relevance of this to poetic tragedy is that already, by the very fact of being in the theatre, we are prepared to accept that "this is a play and not the real thing". Were we, when we go to the theatre, in the habit of believing "these are real people" then the adjustment required when the "real people" began to speak in iambic pentameters or Alexandrines, and to say what no "real person" could ever say, would be too great. But as it is, the difference between the mental attitude required for the two kinds of play is not of kind but only of degree; in both equally we know, and on the one level of consciousness never forget, that the actors are repeating words written for them by someone else; if this awareness does not, when they speak colloquial prose, destroy the illusion on the second level, then it is only one step further in the same direction for the imagination to accept that these words should be poetic verse. All this is, of course, in essentials nothing new; no one has ever more devastatingly demolished the fallacy that we ever mistake a play for the "real thing" than did Samuel Johnson in his *Preface to Shakespeare*. But he simply takes the fact for granted without, as did J. B. Priestley in his broadcast, analysing the state of mind behind it; he, in fact, leaves one dissatisfied, for he speaks as if our awareness that the actors are actors and the stage a stage were the whole truth, and makes no allowance for the second level of consciousness on which we believe the fiction. And this is the difficulty which the phrase "the double level of consciousness" resolves.

CHAPTER V

COMEDY

Comedy is not as easy to define as one might suppose. Laughter—yes, of course, but farce may produce roars of laughter, and there is laughter in Shakespeare's tragedies. And, equally of course, a happy ending, but *The Winter's Tale* and *The Tempest* end happily, yet neither is a comedy.

A comedy is a play which, from beginning to end, is possessed of the comic spirit; if this spirit is lacking no amount of laughter, nor of wedding bells at the end, will make a play a comedy. And this comic spirit consists in a light-hearted way of looking at life, in a choice, from the first scene to the last, of its happier and gayer side, and of what is laughable in human nature to the exclusion of the rest. All art selects—that is its business. Life as we experience it is a confusion of good and evil, joy and sorrow, the serious and the ridiculous, tears and laughter; the strands need to be disentangled if we are to appreciate their significance. And that is what the dramatist does for us, the writer of tragedy showing us the painful elements, the writer of comedy the gay and the ridiculous, a world of laughter in which, even though troubles may occur, they are transitory, and in which, because the evil which makes for tragedy is not present, we know that everything not only will, but must, come right in the end.

So, a comedy is a happy play existing in a world where we can forget the possibility of tragic suffering and where, although tears may be shed, care-free laughter is never far away. There are comedies and comedies, ranging from the laughter all the way of *The Importance of Being Earnest* to the poetic romance of *Twelfth Night* or to the near fantasy of *The Playboy of the Western World.* But always the laughter is light-hearted, with no bitter or sardonic undertones, and this because we know that within the convention of the play we are in a world where no one will get seriously hurt.

Comedy and Farce

In comedy we laugh light-heartedly at the ridiculous. But so, equally, do we in farce. Yet farce is no more comedy than Grand Guignol is tragedy. The difference between the two lies in the kind of ridiculousness that we laugh at.

In farce we laugh at ridiculous happenings and situations, in comedy at ridiculous people. The one, harmless and enjoyable light entertainment as it may be, tells us nothing about human nature; the other, as much as is tragedy, is what Matthew Arnold said that all literature must be, "a criticism of life". Farce is empty of meaning; comedy is as full of meaning as is tragedy. Compare Shakespeare's *The Comedy of Errors*, which, for all its title (for in his time there was only one word for the two kinds of play) is almost pure farce, with any of his later comedies. In *The Comedy of Errors* every laughable situation arises out of the fact that there are two pairs of identical twins, masters and servants, who are, of course, constantly mistaken for each other; no amount of good sense on their parts could have averted the ridiculous confusions; it is not at them that we are laughing, but at what, through no fault of their own, happens to them. At the end we know little more about human nature than we did at the beginning. Contrast with this the sources of our laughter in Shakespeare's true comedies: Malvolio's inordinate vanity, Dogberry's innocent self-importance, Touchstone's running commentary on the follies of his betters, or, to leave the "comics" for the central characters, the self-deceptions of Beatrice and Benedict and their (happy) discomforture when they are ensnared into recognizing the truth about themselves. In all these, laughable as the situations may be, it is not in the situations themselves that the comedy lies, but in the characters' behaviour —their self-revelation—in those situations.

Thoughtful Laughter

So, in comedy we laugh at the ridiculous in human nature. But the recognition of the vanities, the irrationalities, the ludicrous inconsistencies of human behaviour both demands and provokes thought. Hence Meredith's definition in his *Essay on Comedy*: ". . . the test of true comedy is that it shall awaken *thoughtful laughter*" (italics mine). And he goes on to enumerate the ridiculous departures from good sense at which the Spirit of Comedy laughs:

> If you believe that our civilization is founded upon good sense (and it is the first condition of sanity to believe it), you will, when contemplating men, discern a Spirit overhead. . . . Men's future upon earth does not attract it; their honesty and shapeliness in the present does; and whenever they wax out of proportion, overblown, affected, pretentious, bombastical, hypocritical, pedantic, fantastically delicate; whenever it sees them self-deceived or hoodwinked, given to run riot in idolatries, drifting into vanities, congregating in absurdities, planning short-sightedly, plotting dementedly; whenever they are at variance with their professions, and violate the unwritten but perceptible laws binding them in consideration one to another; whenever they offend sound reason, fair justice; are false in humility or mined with conceit, individually or in the bulk—the Spirit overhead will look humanely malign and cast an oblique light on them, followed by volleys of silvery laughter. That is the Comic Spirit.

None of these failings is among the Seven Deadly Sins; all are relatively venial offences, errors of sense rather than of morality, subjects fit for laughter rather than for reprobation. And, although Meredith's list is not all-inclusive—it makes little allowance for the innocently and lovably foolish—nevertheless you will find that the vast majority of the laughable characters created by the great comic writers, and by the lesser ones in so far as they know their business, fall into one or other of his categories.

Head and Heart

So, comedy is addressed to the head: it makes us think. But what of the heart? To what extent should it make us feel?

One answer—a partial one, for although it covers many great comedies it excludes some of the greatest—is, *not at all.* Horace Walpole said: "This world is a comedy to those that think; a tragedy to those that feel." Our intelligence sees folly everywhere; what more ironical folly could be conceived than that man, having, by centuries of scientific progress with the ostensible purpose of bettering the human condition, discovered nuclear energy, should prepare to use his hardly-won discovery to destroy himself and the civilization which he has created? Looked at by a disembodied intelligence without heart it would be "enough to make the gods laugh". And, conversely, the painful humiliation of a rebuffed social climber looked at by a humourless sentimentalist, one who was all heart and no head, would be a subject not for laughter but for pity; to laugh would seem to be heartless cruelty.

So, if Horace Walpole is right, in order that we may enjoy the comic all feeling must be suppressed; the play must be addressed solely to the head and the heart remain untouched. And this—the elimination of all emotional appeal which might inhibit "thoughtful laughter"—has indeed been the central—the classical—tradition of comedy from Aristophanes to Shaw. With such themes as the prospect of nuclear war this elimination is of course impossible if the light-hearted spirit of comedy is to be preserved; if fit subjects for laughter at all they belong to the satirist. Yet that even war itself, given sufficient concentration upon the folly of the war-makers to the exclusion of all reference to the sufferings of the victims, can be turned into laughter with no offence to our feelings is proved by the *Lysistrata* of Aristophanes. It was not that Aristophanes himself was without heart; it was just because he felt so deeply the senseless suffering which war caused that he wrote the play. But he knew that an emotional appeal to the Athenians would be useless; preach to them and they would only become the more determined in their wrong-headedness. But show them to themselves not as knaves but as fools, treat their belligerence not as a crime but as a joke, cut their heroics down to size by ridicule, and their military ardour would dissolve in laughter. As in fact it did: laughter brought them to their senses, they recognized how ridiculously they were behaving—and ended the war.

But it requires a dramatist with a genius akin to that of Aristophanes to make a comedy out of such a potentially tragic theme as war; an error of tact, a lack of sensibility, the slightest reminder of suffering and evil, and the whole thing would become a heartless outrage to our feelings. Such plays are rare. The typical world of comedy is one in which even potential tragedy does not exist, one where the pains involved are no worse than wounded vanity, the exposure of hypocrisy, the deflation of false pretensions—all of which are themselves the fruits of laughable folly. In *L'Avare* Harpagnon is a fool in his avarice; Molière shows us his folly to the exclusion of all else; there is no heartlessness in our laughter, for there is nothing in him with which the heart can sympathize; so with the Morose of Ben Jonson. And in Congreve's *Love for Love* (*The Way of the World* is another matter; I shall return to that later), although in real life his young men's behaviour would deserve serious moral reprobation, they are presented so entirely as young fools in their frustrated attempts at seduction that they become legitimate objects of "thoughtful laughter' and nothing more. And *The Importance of Being Earnest* is pure head and no heart; we are, it is true, told that the young man is in love; he has, in fact, a great deal to say about his passion; but never for one moment are we emotionally involved; his "love" is something "given", a part of the machinery of the play, and no more than a pretext for wit and epigram. And as for the baby in the Gladstone bag: in real life it would be a case of the N.S.P.C.C., but this is not real life; the baby is a mere object, a stage property, there to enable Miss Prism to achieve her comic climax and to bring the play to an end. So with Shaw's comedies (*Pygmalion*, perhaps, excepted): the characters, however much they may hold forth about their feelings, are no more than brilliantly conceived mouthpieces for the irrational beliefs and opinions which Shaw has set out to deflate. We can laugh at them without cruelty, for they have no hearts to break.

The Comedy of Heart

But this, although it is the classical tradition of comedy, is not the only one; there is a comedy of heart, where we can love and pity while we laugh and yet the comic spirit is preserved. Bottom is ridiculous and yet we feel real affection for him; he not only talks about his feelings, he has them; he is no figure of fun but a complete human being. Beatrice and Benedict are pure comedy in their self-deception, yet their love is genuine and deep, not something "given" to be laughed at but something felt. Portia is a woman of passion, appealing to heart as much as, if not more than, to head. And Viola suffers—and we feel her sufferings. And Congreve's Millament: she is not romantically conceived, as are Shakespeare's heroines, but she is no comic abstraction; she is a whole woman, intelligent enough to ridicule the conventions of love-making and marriage, but with a heart which wants her own marriage to be a reality and not a sham.* And *The Playboy of the Western World*: Christie is a dreamer in a world of fantasy, a poetic conception, laughable, of course, but it is laughter of the heart as well as of the head.

Now comes the question: if feeling—sympathy—is there how can the predominantly gay and care-free spirit of comedy be preserved? The world of comedy is a happy world in which we laugh light-heartedly because the very possibility of tragic suffering is absent. If the characters in the play have hearts to be broken how can we laugh at their foolishness and at their misadventures without heartlessness?

The first answer to this question is that, while it is true that the world of the comedy of heart is far nearer to the real world than is that of the comedy of head, still it is an artificial world: it is the real world with *the evil left out*. There may be bad people, as part of the machinery of the plot, though even this is an imperfection; in the most technically perfect comedies misadventure comes through foolishness or accident and not through evil

* For *The Way of the World*, and Millament's Heart, see Bonamy Dobrée's *Restoration Comedy*.

intent. But even where such "bad" people are required to set the plot in motion they must be mere lay-figures, sawdust villains, their evil stated but not fully realized—Duke Frederick and Oliver, for instance, in *As You Like It*; they are there simply as a means of getting the lovers to the forest; their villainy makes no impact upon the imagination. But in the technically perfect romantic comedy there is not even sawdust evil; in *Twelfth Night* there is not a bad person in the whole play. (Sir Toby is a disreputable old rogue, but not to be taken seriously.) Viola's unhappiness (and she is, for a time, very unhappy) is occasioned solely by mischance and misunderstanding; no one wishes her ill; all that is required to make her happy is that her disguise should be removed. It is true that there are some (Lamb among them) who see an element of cruelty in the treatment of Malvolio, but, after all, he suffered nothing worse than the pains of wounded vanity, and that he brought upon himself by his inordinate conceit. *The Merchant of Venice* is another matter, but it only goes to prove the rule; it is, although a great play, as a comedy faulty. Shylock is evil, and fully realized evil, a complete human being, and, to the extent that he dominates the play, he shatters the comic spirit; the play falls into two parts, the Belmont theme romantic comedy, Shylock and the bond potential tragedy; Shakespeare can only bring the two together in the trial scene by so weakening Shylock's character that we forget his earlier greatness.* What, it seems, may have happened was that Shakespeare, wishing to exploit the box-office appeal of the anti-semitism which we know was rampant at that time,† planned a play with a merely sawdust comic Jew as a part of the machinery of the plot, but that once his imagination got to work Shylock came alive as an evil but suffering human being, a member of a persecuted race. He then had the choice: either to keep Shylock and wreck the unity of the play, or to reject one of his greatest

* For Shakespeare's evident awareness that Shylock and the spirit of Belmont are incompatible see Granville-Barker, *Prefaces to Shakespeare,* Series 11.

† Anti-semitism, always endemic in England at that period, became epidemic after the execution of the Jew Lopez on an almost certainly unfounded charge of attempting to poison Queen Elizabeth.

creations. Fortunately he chose the former course, and gave us Shylock. But nevertheless the play, as a comedy, is faulty. The one dramatist who successfully introduces evil into a comedy is Molière in *Tartuffe*. But then many people question whether *Tartuffe* is a comedy at all, or whether in it Molière has not created a new dramatic genre transcending categories.

A second rule which must be observed if the comic spirit is to be preserved is that, although feeling is present, it must go *thus far and no further*; never must a character be allowed even within sight of heart-break. Viola is unhappy—yes, very unhappy, but not to the point where she cannot exchange back-chat with Feste. Rosalind faints at the sight of Orlando's blood, but we know, even though she does not, that the play is approaching its happy ending, and in any case the whole tone of the scene is so light-hearted that we do not take her faint too seriously. Hero in *Much Ado About Nothing* is another matter; if, as is generally assumed, she passionately loves Claudio, then her falling unconscious and apparently dead when he denounces her is out of key and destroys the comic spirit; but this would only go to show that Shakespeare had, not for the first time, made a technical mistake. But in fact the fault here probably lies with the critics and not with Shakespeare; if we read the earlier scenes carefully we shall find that Hero has given no sign that she loves Claudio; all she wants is to make a good match with a handsome young man; if this reading is correct she swoons not from a broken heart but from humiliation and wounded vanity, and the scene is perfectly in key with the spirit of comedy.

And a third requirement if the comic spirit is to be preserved is that the whole tone of the play, from the first scene to the last, shall say to us, clearly and unmistakably, "This is a comedy!" And because we are all familiar with the comic convention we shall then know from first to last that the troubles will be transitory, that we are in a world where no hearts will be broken, nor anyone seriously hurt, and that everything will come right in the end. As long as this tone is sustained our laughter can be care-free even though our hearts may be engaged. In Christopher Fry's

Venus Observed—not a great but still a good comedy—the Duke and Perpetua, trapped in a burning house with, apparently, no means of escape, seem to be on the point of death. For a moment one may fear for their lives, but only for a moment; one has only to remember the tone of the earlier scenes to know that as good a craftsman as Fry will turn the situation to laughter. And, sure enough, the butler appears and effects a laughable rescue.

The Comedy of Manners

The bombastic militarism at which Aristophanes laughs in the *Lysistrata* is a universal folly; so are Malvolio's vanity, Dogberry's self-importance, Harpagnon's avarice, Tartuffe's hypocrisy; the setting of each play is that of its own time and place, but the same follies are found always and everywhere. But certain comic dramatists have taken as their butt, not these universal follies, but others peculiar to their own day and to the society in which they live, foolish fashions, and have written what is called the Comedy of Manners. *Les Précieuses Ridicules* and *Les Femmes Savantes* are comedies of manners; both make fun of ephemeral affectations which today are as dead as the dodo. And our Restoration Comedy laughs not, as did the Elizabethan, at universal human nature but at certain specific false conventions of London society in the latter part of the seventeenth and the early eighteenth centuries. (The term Restoration is misleading; *The Way of the World* was written in 1700.) Dryden in *Marriage à la Mode* is ridiculing the convention of fashionable society in his day according to which adultery was "smart", marital fidelity dowdy; Congreve in *Love for Love* exposes the folly of the sexual licence which, again, was considered "smart", and in *The Way of the World* of an ephemeral fashion in love-making and marriage. And Sheridan's plays are comedies of manners; they too laugh at contemporary social conventions, affectations and fashions. And not only are the "follies" those of a particular time and place, they are confined to a social class, the "mannered". Now, if this were all, the plays would have been as ephemeral as the fashions which gave them birth; they would have gone the way of all topical jokes. Yet all have lived. And they have lived because, while ostensibly ridiculing nothing but some passing "craze", all have in fact gone deeper; they ridicule not only the"crazes" themselves, but the kind of people who follow every fashion, however foolish it may be. And wherever fashions exist—that is to say, in any relatively wealthy and sophisticated urban society—such people will always be with us. The fashions may change, but the desire to conform to them remains. The Comedy of Manners can thus, for all its topicality, be universal.

The Comedy of Humours

The Comedy of Humours was the creation of Ben Jonson, and as a dramatic genre died with him, although the individual "humour" survived to re-appear in certain eighteenth-century novels. Ben Jonson explains the principle in the Induction to *Every Man Out of His Humour* (Asper's speech beginning, "O, I crave pardon; I had lost my thoughts. / Why, humour as 'tis *ens*, we thus define it.") Briefly, Ben Jonson takes the word "humour" from the medical doctrine of the four humours, but uses it metaphorically to indicate any obsessive passion (e.g. avarice) which dominates the person so

> . . . that it doth draw
> All his affects, his spirits, and his powers,
> In their confluctions, all to run one way. . . . .

And so completely is the character in a Comedy (or, later, in a novel) of Humours identified with his obsession that the character himself has become a "Humour". A humour is not intended to be a complete human being; he is little more than a personification of one single obsessive folly. But, given Ben Jonson's genius, the method does provide a means, akin to that of the scientist who isolates a single element which in nature would never be found alone, of showing that folly pure and unadulterated. Morose is a humour, so is Sir Epicure Mammon in *The Alchemist*. (Note the descriptive names; wherever such names are found in later drama or in the novel the character will be, to a greater or less extent, a humour.) But Ben Jonson himself as time went on found the method a straight-jacket; even in *Every Man in His Humour* Bobadil breaks the mould of the boaster, and becomes a many-sided human being. And in his later plays the humours become fewer.

So much for the art of comedy and its different kinds. But as a postscript here are two notes, the first a useful pair of definitions, the second on a kind of laughter which is sometimes mistakenly called "comic", but which has nothing of the spirit of comedy.

Note 1. Humour and Wit

Both humour and wit have their place in comedy; both (whatever Meredith may, in his *Essay on Comedy*, say to the contrary) can provoke thoughtful laughter. Humour predominates in Shakespeare; Molière is both humorous and witty; Congreve and Wilde are witty.

Humour works *immediately* and *directly*; no thought is necessary in order to see the ludicrous incongruity of the situation or of the words; laughter comes spontaneously; if thought is to be provoked, *we laugh first and think afterwards*. (That is one of the reasons why Meredith, with his bias in favour of wit, excludes humour from his "thoughtful laughter".) On the lowest level a red-nosed comedian or a piece of slap-stick appeal to our sense of humour; they look funny. But this kind of humour belongs not to comedy but to farce; it gives us nothing to think about. But when ludicrous behaviour or words are not only immediately laughable in themselves but reveal something laughable in the character of the actor or speaker, then, as much as does wit, they belong to comedy: we laugh first at what we see or hear, then we think, and then we laugh again—thoughtfully. The nurse's garrulity in *Romeo and Juliet* is funny in itself, so are Bottom's boastings and Dogberry's malapropisms; so is Malvolio when he soliloquizes and we watch Sir Toby and his fellow conspirators overhearing every word, and so are Monsieur Jourdain's attempts to be a gentleman. But the true comedy of all these lies not in what the characters do, however ludicrous, but in that in themselves which makes them do it, and to appreciate this requires thought. But nevertheless laughter comes first.

Wit, on the other hand, works in two stages: *we think first and laugh afterwards*, and, in contradistinction to humour, until we have thought there is nothing to laugh at. For wit plays with the incongruities not of behaviour but of ideas; we must grasp the idea before we see the incongruity. Sir Henry Wotton, James I's ambassador in Venice, defined an ambassador as "an honest man who lies abroad for the good of his country". Here first one must remember the two meanings of "to lie abroad", contrast what one meaning (to live abroad, or to sleep abroad) tells us that an ambassador ostensibly does, with what the other tells us is his actual business (to tell lies), and then, to get the full savour, one must go back to the words, "an honest man"; then, and not till then, comes the laughter. The process is quite complex. A quick-witted person may, it is true, "see the point" so almost instantaneously as to be unaware of the mental processes involved, yet even so the laughter has come at one remove—thought first, laughter afterwards.

Note 2. Laughter in Tragedy

Comic laughter belongs to a world with the evil left out. What then of the laughter in Shakespeare's tragedies? The neo-classicists of course condemned it: laughter to them was incompatible with tragic seriousness and destroyed the emotional unity of the play. And were the laughter in Shakespeare's tragedies the care-free laughter of comedy they would be right. But, the Nurse in *Romeo and Juliet* apart, it is not.

For there are in Shakespeare's plays two kinds of laughter: the light-hearted laughter of comedy, and a bitter, sardonic or ironic laughter with tragic overtones. It is the latter which we find in his mature tragedies. The Porter in *Macbeth*, the Grave-diggers in *Hamlet*, the Clown who brings the asp to Cleopatra, have nothing in common with comedy; their humour is macabre, providing not, as is sometimes said, "comic relief", but tragic irony. The Porter, in his drunkenness, plays the part of the porter at hell-gate; Macbeth, within, is in hell. The Grave-diggers ignorantly moralizing upon death are an ironic commentary upon the tragedy which, uncomprehendingly, they are witnessing. Most ironic—and touching—of all, perhaps, is the Clown who innocently brings Cleopatra her death.

The apparent exception is Juliet's nurse. She is, indeed, a character of comedy; the laughter she provokes has no tragic or ironic overtones. But Shakespeare's treatment of her, and the place which he gives her in the play, far from invalidating, only goes to confirm that comic laughter has no place in tragedy. For *Romeo and Juliet*, an early and immature play, is not pure tragedy; J. W. Mackail, in his *An Approach to Shakespeare*, calls it a romance with a tragic ending. And in Act V, where romance turns to tragedy, the nurse does not appear. In pure tragedy the end is, from first to last, inevitable; given that hero in that situation there is no way out, and from the opening of the play we know it. A romance, on the other hand, is a serious story or play set in a potentially tragic world in which, however, good triumphs over evil and tragedy is averted. (Shakespeare's last three plays, *Cymbeline*, *The Winter's Tale* and *The Tempest* are thus romances.) Now, in *Romeo and Juliet* right up to the end of Act IV there is a way out; had not the sonnet which precedes the play as Prologue told us that they were "star-crossed", we should see no reason why the lovers should not survive their troubles and live happily ever after. Juliet's plan seems fool-proof, and would have been had it not been for the mere accident of Friar John's quarantine; it is only with the non-delivery of the letter that tragedy becomes inevitable. And from then onwards the Nurse is forgotten. When, in Act IV, she thinks that Juliet is dead but we know that she is not, she can indulge in a fit of comic hysterics. But imagine the effect if she had re-appeared at the tomb and staged a comic turn by the bodies of the dead lovers! The Porter, the Grave-diggers and the Clown can be present at the very heart of the tragedy because they are figures not of comedy but of tragic irony; the Nurse, who belongs to the world of comedy, cannot.

There is, indeed, a class of plays which set out to juxtapose true comedy and tragedy, the so-called tragi-comedies of the seventeenth century. In these there are two parallel plots, one comic and the other tragic, the scenes generally alternating between the two; Fletcher's *The Humorous Lieutenant* is a typical example. But one has only to read the plays to discover the tastelessness of the juxtaposition of the two moods. The use of the term "tragi-comedy" to describe an incident in real life or in fiction which at the same time produces laughter and pity is different; it is never used of a situation which is tragic in Aristotle's sense of the word, but only of one in which the pain, though genuine, is of a relatively minor order.

CHAPTER VI

CLASSICAL AND ROMANTIC

NOTICE the title of this chapter: Classical and Romantic, not Classic*ism* and Romantic*ism*. The two pairs of words are not synonymous, and confusion often arises through failure to distinguish between them. One can, it is true, in general say that the classicist is classical, the romanticist romantic, and in this chapter I shall often so describe them. But the reverse does not hold good, and if we limit the meaning of the word "classical" to classicism and of "romantic" to romanticism, then many of the most essentially classical and romantic writers and artists will be excluded. The words in the first pair designate two attitudes of mind towards life and its expression in the arts which have probably existed ever since man began to think about life and to express himself in art, and one or other of which has tended to predominate at any given period, even if no one at that time stopped to think which of the two he was. (So little, in fact, did they think about it that it was not until the 'isms came into existence that words were coined to describe the two ways of looking.) The second pair, the 'isms, on the other hand, refer to two specific movements in relatively modern times in each of which one or the other of these two attitudes to life and to art came to be formulated as an ideology, as a creed or cult, with its manifestoes, its body of doctrine, its evangelists—and a name. And each of these movements was a *revival*—a conscious attempt to return to the art forms and what its adherents believed (though often mistakenly) to be the spirit of an earlier period in which that way of looking at things seemed to them to have reached its supreme manifestation. The classical spirit had existed, and expressed itself in the arts, intermittently all through history; classicism was born of the Renaissance rediscovery of Greek, and the desire to imitate Greek and Roman, literature and art. There have always been romantics (even in "classical" Greece); romanticism is the name given to the late eighteenth- and early nineteenth-century reaction against classicism and (though it came to include very much else) was in its origins very largely an attempt to return to what was believed to have been the spirit of the Middle Ages. In this chapter I shall treat of the classical and romantic attitudes of mind and then go on to the 'isms.

But first must come:

A Preliminary Warning

The words classical and romantic are not pigeon-holes; they are not the names of self-contained categories into one or other of which every individual writer, artist, or period can be securely tucked away. The words stand, not for categories of artists or periods, but for two attitudes of mind, ways of looking at life and art, temperamental sympathies and affinities, both of which may, to a greater or less extent, be present in the same individual or period. Cecil Day Lewis, in *The Poetic Image* (p. 30), having just quoted the classicist Sidney as saying something purely romantic and the ultra-romantic Shelley something typically classical, goes on:

> We must resist the temptation, as strong now as ever it was, of dividing poets into teams and making them play against each other—alas, poor critic, having to referee a match in which the players are constantly fraternizing, exchanging jerseys, running in the wrong direction and turning the rules to anarchy.

The words must be retained—they are indispensable—but *always to describe the classical or romantic element in a writer, and never with the implication that that writer is all of a piece.* It is true that in the case of many writers one or the other element is so predominant that we can, and do, usefully indicate that predominance by describing him by one or other of the terms. There is a fundamental difference between the philosophies of life of Racine and Wordsworth, and even though Racine may have had his romantic moments, and though Wordsworth had most certainly retained a saving strain of rationalism from his eighteenth-century classical education, that difference can only be indicated by describing Racine as classical, Wordsworth as romantic. But the use of the words does not exclude the possibility of the presence of the other element. And when we come to other writers such as Goethe and Byron we cannot label then even to this extent. Both belonged to the Romantic Movement (Byron in fact, by those who know only his earlier poetry and the more sensational facts of his life, is looked upon as the very type of the romantic), yet both had such strong classical affinities that Goethe completely, and Byron in a large degree, as they matured became "classical". So with periods: a so-called classical period may reveal a romantic strain, a romantic one a classical. So remember—always—that the words stand not for self-contained categories of writers or periods but for a more or less predominant tendency in any given writer or period. And used in this sense the two words are essential, for these tendencies exist and can only be identified if we give them names. As I proceed I shall be obliged to say "the romantic"—or, as the case may be, "the classical"—"writer or artist believes so-and-so", but always it will be with the implied qualification, "*in so far as he is romantic or classical*". I shall be defining the classical or romantic element in him, and not implying that in any one individual writer or artist the other element may not be present.

One further preliminary before we come to define the two attitudes of mind:

The Words Classical and Romantic

Classical. The word dates from the Renaissance and comes from the confusion of two Latin words: *classicus*=of the highest class or rank, and *classis*=a class (at school). The Greek and Latin were considered to be the only first-class literatures; at the same time, they were the only literatures taught "in class". Thus "classic" came to mean Greek and Latin, irrespective of which of the Latin words it was derived from.

But the adjective "classical" is today used in three main senses:

(1) To describe everything—language, mythology, philosophy, art, architecture—belonging to the great ages of the cultures of Greece and Rome.

(2) As a loose term for what, if we want specifically to distinguish between (1) and (2), we call classicist or, alternatively, neo-classical: any work of art (architecture, sculpture, drama, epic, etc.) produced in imitation *of the forms* of Greek or Roman art.

(3) To describe any work of art which embodies the Greek *spirit*, even if it does not, and often cannot, imitate Greek or Roman forms. In this sense Haydn's music is classical although he could not imitate the forms of Greek music, for none has been preserved.

The adjective "classical" and the noun "classic" are, however, also used in a different and confusing sense:

(1) "A" classic, in the sense in which the word is used in the O.U.P. series The World's Classics, a collection of reprints which includes, besides the classical, all the great romantic writers. The word is here used in the sense of *classicus*, "of the highest rank"; we no longer rank Greek and Latin literature above all others; a romantic work can stand as high as a classical, and hence can be called "*a* classic". But it does not thereby become "classical". This use of the word is of course totally irrelevant to the theme of this chapter.

(2) Classical music. This has two meanings: (a) music which has the classical, as opposed to the romantic, spirit (cf. (3) above); (b) "high-class" music, whether classical or romantic in spirit (cf. "A" classic), generally with the added implication, "has proved its worth by surviving the test of time". In this sense the music of Brahms is "classical", and it is even legitimate to speak of "classical jazz". But (b), like "a" classic, has, obviously,

no bearing upon the distinction between "classical" and "romantic".

Romantic. The word Romance originally indicated a language derived from the Roman (Latin), especially that of Provence. It was in the Provençal language that the Trouvères wrote their poems of what we now call "romantic" love: the name of the language became attached to the subject-matter, and was then extended to include tales of chivalry and of the marvellous. By the seventeenth century "romantic" had become a pejorative, "fantastic", "incredible". It was the Romantic Movement which gave it its present meaning, which includes its earlier meanings of romantic love and of the marvellous but, as you will see, embraces very much more.

These preliminaries disposed of, we now come to the main theme:

The Classical and Romantic Attitudes of Mind

First, two visual symbols which better than anything else, I think, embody the fundamental difference between the classical and romantic attitudes to life and to the arts: visualize (a) the Parthenon (you will certainly be familiar with pictures of it), and (b) any Gothic Cathedral which you know. For (b) the example which I am using is Chartres, and if you know it or can obtain a picture of it so much the better. But any other, though differing in detail, will illustrate the same principles.

(a) *The classical ideal.* The Parthenon. Notice two things: (1) the whole is *self-contained within an unbroken bounding line*; and (2) its beauty lies in *the perfect proportion of the parts to the whole.* These characteristics we can see for ourselves today, but there is a third significant point which no existing Greek temple in its mutilated state reveals: the dark interior was no more than a storehouse for treasures offered to the god or goddess; the altar stood outside; it was here, in the clear Mediterranean sunlight, that the priest offered sacrifice. And so to complete the picture you must add (3) the now lost open-air altar. But to return to (1) and (2): these two points are interrelated. Parts cannot be brought into proportion to the whole unless the exact size and shape of the whole have first been determined. And once the parts and the whole have been created in perfect proportion to each other, nothing can be added to or taken away from the whole without destroying this relationship; hence the *predetermined* bounding line. Notice, further, that I said that the whole was *self-contained* and the bounding line *unbroken*; the line is unbroken because all the beauty, all that the artist has to say to us, lies *within* that line, and therefore our eye must not be allowed to stray beyond it.

The classical ideal is *perfection* within *limits*. And each of the italicized words is equally important. For without limits you cannot have perfection, which by definition is wholeness, completeness, unimprovableness, something to which nothing can be added and from which nothing can be taken away without destroying its perfection. One of the symbols of perfection is the circle: you can draw a big circle or a small one, but once it is drawn you cannot make it bigger by adding a bulge, or smaller by cutting off a segment; if you do it will cease to be a circle at all. Hence if your aim is perfection—completeness, wholeness—in any of the arts, you must, however well aware you may be of possible beauties beyond your self-imposed limits, draw a bounding line somewhere and be content to stay within it.

This is the spirit of Greek—and of all classical—art. True, the Greeks as a people were far from "classical" in temperament; they were, in fact, exceptionally individualistic, intolerant of restraint and discipline, and given to breaking bounds. Nevertheless, in their art, possibly just because their individualism had taught them the dangers of unrestricted liberty, they did choose to work within self-imposed limits and thus produced not only an architecture but a whole culture of which the Parthenon may be taken as the symbol. In all their arts, and even in their philosophy, the same principle is at work. Take sculpture: each sculptor pursued one accepted type of human beauty, each one trying, not to break the mould and explore new possibilities, but to do the traditional thing more and more perfectly. And even the pose of the figure must be contained within a bounding line; a statue in which the arms point outwards is not classical but Hellenistic.* So with drama: the limitations set by its religious origin were accepted as given; the form of the play and the treatment of the myths might develop and evolve, but always within the bounding line drawn by tradition. And philosophy limited itself to the nature of man and his right relationships with other men and (because no distinction was made between philosophy and what we now call the natural sciences) the workings of the physical universe. In other words—and here we come to the significance of the sunlight which illuminated altar and worshippers—it confined itself to the *knowable*, to what could be comprehended and ordered by *the light of reason*, leaving the mysterious severely alone.

For the Greeks—and this is fundamental to their view of life—more than any other people believed in the supremacy of reason. And what is unknowable, or only partially knowable, cannot be reasoned about. They recognized, of course, as every highly imaginative and creative people must, the existence of the supra-rational, of the mysteries above the reach of reason, but those they left to the gods. The wise man was content to confine his speculations to what his reason could comprehend. True, their philosophers and scientists, with their insatiable intellectual curiosity and passionate thirst for truth, were constantly pushing further and further afield the frontier between the known and the unknown, and hence extending the range within which reason could do its work. But still the frontier, the bounding line, remained: on the one side the known, clarity, exactitude, mathematical precision, on the other the intangible, the incomprehensible, the mysterious, the sphere not of man but of the gods. One might meditate upon these, as did the tragic drama-

* For this I am indebted to Sir Kenneth Clark's *The Nude*. But there are exceptions: Zeus throwing a thunderbolt (Nat. Mus., Athens) has extended arms. Hellenistic=of the post-classical period, the 4th Century B.C. onwards.

tists upon the mystery of human suffering, but to attempt to penetrate them was the supreme folly, *hubris*, the desire to transcend human limitations and to aspire to the knowledge and power which belonged to the gods alone.

Now to return to the Parthenon. In its perfect clarity of form, the lucidity of its mathematical proportions, and in its unbroken bounding line which forbids the eye to stray into the beyond, it is a rational building. Mystery is there, of course, in the sense that any supreme work of art is mysterious, but the mystery lies not in what it says to us but in the inexplicable miracle of the creative imagination which has said it. That—the creative imagination itself—is always something beyond and above the reach of reason, and no one knew this better than the Greeks themselves; that is why they believed that no artist could work without the inspiration of the Muses. But in the Parthenon—as in all great classical art—it is reason which has imposed the proportioned, unified and self-contained pattern without which it could not have achieved the wholeness which is its perfection.

So to sum up, the Greek—and classical—ideal is *perfection within limits*, and this ideal is achieved by *the imagination controlled and disciplined by reason.**

(b) *The romantic spirit*. The Gothic cathedral. As I have said, I am taking Chartres as my example. Should you be visualizing another cathedral I leave you to identify the relevant features for yourself.

In three essential points you will notice that the Gothic Cathedral is the antithesis of the Parthenon: (1) *It is not enclosed within an unbroken bounding line:* spires and pinnacles *break through* and *lead our eye upward to infinity*. And even in the interior, although it is true that the vaulting sets a limit, every line aspires, soars upwards, from earth to heaven. And (2) *it was not planned as a*

* Despite inevitable, though I hope not too misleading, over-simplification, my debt in this section to Sir Maurice Bowra's *The Greek Experience* will be evident to anyone who has read the book. It is essential reading for anyone who wishes to pursue the subject.

whole; as we see it, it has evolved from century to century, each generation adding, changing, "improving".* To take the west front of Chartres: the starting point is the twelfth-century South Clocher, with the Porte Royal and three windows above it. These, it is true, were designed almost as a proportioned whole—but even so, not quite, for the portal was completed before the width of the clocher was determined upon, and had to be slightly mutilated when the latter was placed beside it. Then came the thirteenth century: the façade was heightened and the great rose-window placed above the three existing ones; the clocher was dwarfed by the disproportionate height of the façade. Finally, three centuries later came the North Clocher, in a different style of architecture from and higher than, and thus out of balance with, the South one. And if we go from the west front to the North and South Porches, these were after-thoughts, added after their respective Portals were already completed, and yet they and their Portals together are among the great glories of the cathedral. And (3) the interior, if, as at Chartres, the original stained glass has been preserved, is dark, mysterious, illuminated only by the jewel-like glow of the windows. (Should the cathedral you are visualizing have lost its stained glass you must try in imagination to restore it.)

Now to sum up the contrast between the Gothic cathedral and the Parthenon: (1) instead of the whole contained within a bounding line which forbids the eye to stray beyond itself, spires and pinnacles and, in the interior, soaring pillars and vaults point upwards to infinity; (2) the absence of a predetermined unity of design rules out the possibility of symmetrically proportioned wholeness and unimprovableness—that is to say of perfection in the sense that the Parthenon is perfect; and, finally, (3) the interior, the place of congregational worship, is in mysterious semi-darkness, in contrast to the rational clarity of the Greek sunlit altar. The medieval mind, unlike the Greek, lived in a

* Even in Salisbury, the most nearly "all-of-one-piece" of the English cathedrals, the two western bays of the nave were not a part of the original design.

world of the *supernatural, of illimitable mystery, of aspiration towards an unknown and unknowable infinity.*

This is not to say that the Middle Ages, any more than the Greeks, were all of a piece; the belief that they were was one of the major mistakes of the Romantic Movement. Scholastic theology was inspired by Aristotelian logic. (Aristotle himself is one of the sages carved on the Porte Royal at Chartres.) There is a Greek mathematical precision in the proportions of the individual parts of Chartres, though no over-all design for the whole. Even the columnar figures on the Porte Royal suggest that the sculptor must have been familiar with early Greek sculpture.* And, further, although the soul must aspire to heaven, transcending earthly limitations, it was far from free to do so in its own way; it was the Church alone who knew the way and whose discipline set strict bounds to the individual's freedom. Yet, nevertheless, despite all this the medieval mind did differ fundamentally from the Greek in its constant awareness of the supernatural and its striving towards infinity and the unknowable. Earth, with its familiar measurable "knownness", was but a temporary abiding place; heaven, the unknown and the immeasurable, was the goal towards which the soul must aspire. And even earth was impinged upon by heaven in miracles and marvels. It is this aspiration from the known to the unknown, from the bounded finite to the unbounded infinite, from earth to heaven, which is, whatever qualifications one may be obliged to make when dealing with medieval society as a whole, the spirit embodied in a Gothic cathedral.

And this spirit is romantic. The romantic is at heart an explorer of mysteries, of the transcendental, of the beyond. Whereas to the classical temperament a bounding line says: "Stop! Cross me at your peril!", or, to put it more crudely, "Don't bite off more than you can chew", to the romantic it is a challenge, a frontier to be crossed in order to discover the mysteries which lie beyond it. And once the mystery becomes

* For this I am indebted to Sir Kenneth Clark's 1961/2 Slade Lectures.

unmysterious, known, explained, it loses its charm, and further frontiers must be crossed with fresh mysteries beyond them. The essence of romance is in the Ancient Mariner's:

> We were *the first* that ever burst
> *Into that silent sea.*

But the last word is Wordsworth's:

> . . . Our being's heart and home
> Is *with infinitude* and only there.

Wordsworth—and most of his fellow romanticists would have agreed with him—has carried the principle embodied in the soaring lines, the ever-present possibility of growth and the dimly-lighted interior, to its ultimate limit. Not every romantic aspires so high. But always, in so far as the romantic element is present, there will be the aspiration towards the transcendental, the extreme. The conception of "romantic love", which was the creation of the Trouvères and which has run through European poetry and romantic fiction ever since their day, is one of transcendent love, boundless love, love which exists in its own right and is its own self-justification whatever may be the dictates of reason—what love might be were life made for falling in love and for nothing else. So with the "romantic hero". Cervantes in *Don Quixote* was, of course, burlesquing the code of chivalry, but nevertheless by his very exaggeration and by carrying the romantic principle to its logical conclusion he has isolated its essence: the aspiration towards an ideal of transcendent, boundless, infinite honour, generosity and selfless devotion, however impossible may be its attainment in this imperfect world. Don Quixote was a madman, but every romantic hero (in real life as well as in fiction), however sane he may be, has in him something of the quixotic urge to transcend human limitations and to pursue his dream even though reason may tell him that it is unattainable. So with every manifestation of the romantic spirit: it is never content with the known, the attainable; its urge always is to break bounds. And wherever you find this spirit, whether in Classical Greece or Rome, or in the world today, its possessor is a romantic.

The 'isms

As I have already said, the mark of the 'isms—Classicism and Romanticism—is that both were *ideologies*. And this because, unlike the cultures of Greece and of the Middle Ages, both were conscious and deliberate breaks with tradition. In Greece the classical principle of perfection within limits was taken for granted; even though individuals with an inborn romantic urge might assert their right to be different, it seemed to the vast majority so obviously the right and natural way of producing a work of art that there was no need to argue about it. True, there was plenty of theorizing about literature and art (Aristotle wrote the *Poetics*), but this theorizing was *within the tradition*; there was no need to formulate or codify or justify the tradition itself. So with the Middle Ages: people felt like that; they took it for granted—even though of course many found this earth a pleasant place to live in—that heaven was their goal and that, even if they did not, at least they ought to aspire to it. And they *liked* tales of the supernatural; it did not occur to them to justify their liking or to condemn those who did not share it. And just because they did not need to codify what they felt in their blood and in their bones, they saw no inconsistency between what we would now call the "romantic" urge towards the mysterious and the illimitable and the classical rationality of Aristotelian logic.

But the classicists and the romanticists were not working within a living tradition; both were trying to *revive* an earlier tradition (or at least what they believed that tradition to have been) which was unfamiliar and alien to the majority of their contemporaries. True, in each case external circumstances had prepared the soil: the world—or at least the younger generation—was becoming restless, disillusioned with things as they were, hungry for change; a swing of the pendulum was, in the long run, inevitable. But the actual revolutions of taste were brought about by a spearhead of enthusiasts, of propagandists, working against the tradition into which they had been born and passionately determined to convert the world to their new creed. And a creed, if it is to be preached, must be formulated, made explicit and given its philosophical justification. Nothing can be taken for granted; a reason must be found for everything, and all doctrinal aberrations become heresy. Which is to say that that which in a traditional culture is intuitive and hence is flexible must become crystallized as an ideology.

Classicism

This, of course, was the offspring of the Renaissance rediscovery of, and intoxication with, Greek philosophy, literature and art. To the Renaissance classicist everything Greek (and to a lesser extent Roman) became a standard of civilized perfection; what was not Greek or Roman was barbarous. There was one—and only one—way of creating a work of art: the classical. And because he had not, as had the Greeks, the classical tradition "in his bones", the only way to be sure of doing the thing correctly was to deduce from his models a set of *Rules*. This—the reduction of everything to rule—is the distinctive mark of classicism as compared with the intuitive and traditional Greek classical. Because Homer—and Virgil in imitation of him—had constructed their epics in a certain way therefore every epic must have the same construction, down to the smallest detail. Because Greek plays (for reasons of which the classicists were ignorant) generally had their action limited to one place and to a period of twenty-four hours, therefore every play must observe what (quite unjustifiably) came to be called the Unities of Place and Time. And so with every other rule which could be deduced from Greek and Roman practice.

The rules were innumerable; each art and branch of literature had its own; it is impossible, and unnecessary, to enumerate them here. All that is necessary to remember is their existence, and why they existed. But among them there are two which stand in a class apart from the rest; they are not, in fact, rules at all in the sense in which "The Three Unities" is a rule; they are rather statements of principle which are fundamental to the classicist—and, for that matter, the classical, for both are borrowed from the Greeks—aesthetic. These it is essential for us to know if we are to understand not only neo-classical art but the Romantic reaction against it.

(a) *The General, not the Particular.* Aristotle states the principle (*Poetics*, section 9):

> . . . The poet's function is to describe not the thing that has happened, but a kind of thing that might happen . . . hence poetry is something more philosophic and of graver import than history, since its statements are of the nature rather of *universals*, whereas those of history are *singulars*. By a universal statement I mean one as to what *such or such a kind of man will probably or necessarily say or do*.

What the Greeks assumed, and the classicists turned into a dogma, was that the imaginative artist's business was not with the eccentricities which differentiate one individual from another of the same type, but with the universal characteristics which all men of a certain type have in common. They were concerned with human nature as it is, always and everywhere, not with the individual inconsistencies and aberrations from the norm which may occur once and once only. If a tragic hero falls through pride, then the fact (which Shakespeare might well have told us) that he also loved cats is totally irrelevant, for cat-loving is not a universal mark of over-proud men. So of a coward or a fool: what he has in common with other cowards or fools and not what distinguishes him from them is the dramatic or narrative poet's theme. And not only the poet's, but the visual artist's. If you want to paint or sculpt a beautiful woman you select what she has in common with other beautiful women of her type and omit what is peculiar to herself; in this way you are universalizing her, not depicting one single individual but creating a type of what is beautiful for all time.

And this last example leads on to the second, and closely related, principle:

(b) *Idealization.* It is in the visual arts rather than in literature that this principle is most evident. For in drama or narrative poetry the characters must have faults (cf. Aristotle's hero of tragedy: "a man not pre-eminently virtuous and just . . ."); though even here there is a heightening of the noble qualities; they are on the grand scale, and all petty failings are omitted. And in the lesser classicists, who worked by rule and rule alone, there did develop a tendency (Aristotle notwithstanding) to idealize to the point of making their characters inhumanly faultless. (For the absurdity of this kind of idealization read Dryden's preface, *Of Heroic Plays.*) But in classical sculpture and painting the principle is absolute. The Greek and neo-classical sculptors and painters aimed at representing the human form not as it is but as it would be had Nature done her work perfectly. They assumed the existence of a norm of beauty from which every individual is, to a greater or less extent, an aberration. And the artist's business was not to reproduce these aberrations but to discover the norm, to create an ideal of beauty to which even the most beautiful individual is but an approximation. No Greek Venus is a representation of any individual woman; all are idealizations with Nature's mistakes corrected. And the classicists extended this principle from the human form to nature. Claude (and in this respect he is a pure classicist, however much his romantic imagination may have modified his art in other ways) in his landscapes did not set out to represent the scene as Nature had made it; instead he painted it as it might have been had Nature been a classical artist. His hills are perfectly balanced one against another; not a tree has been misshapen by wind or weather, and they are grouped as a landscape gardener of genius might have grouped them.

Romanticism

As rules are the mark of classicism, so *rejection of rule* is the mark of the Romantic Movement. Rules had become a tyranny, a strait-jacket, inhibiting the free play of the imagination; as always happens in a revolutionary movement, the pendulum swung to the opposite extreme: all rules were evil and must be abandoned in favour of unrestricted liberty to follow the imagination wherever it might lead. Hence the difficulty of summing up neatly the various manifestations of romanticism. The essence of classicism was that every classicist was in agreement, and it is comparatively easy to define that about which they agreed. But once the one rule about which everyone agrees is that there must be no rule—that every creative artist must be a law unto himself—then there is no telling how any individual may not use his liberty. All that one can do is to give a list of "either/ors".

Nevertheless, though there were no rules, there were certain principles about which every romanticist, in so far as he was one (but do not forget the artist's habit of playing for both teams), was in agreement. And of these the first was *the autonomy of the imagination.* And this was something new in the history of thought. Every creative artist has always known (if he has thought about the matter at all) that art *is born of* the imagination: no imagination, no art. The classical Greeks and the great classicists knew this just as well as did any romantic. (For the classical Dryden's conception of the imagination read T. S. Eliot's *The Use of Poetry and the Use of Criticism*; you will find that no one knew better than he that the imagination is the only source of poetry.) But whereas the Greeks and the classicists believed that the imagination gives only the raw material of poetry and that reason (or judgement, as Dryden calls it) must assess that material, prune it of its irrationalities and of all that is irrelevant, and consciously mould it into a work of art, to the romanticists the imagination was not only the source of all poetry but its sole creator, and, in extreme cases such as that of Shelley, not only of poetry but of civilization, morality and religion. It came to be regarded as an "inner light", the divine element in man, the only faculty by which he could penetrate through appearances and apprehend reality. It thus transcended reason and owed no allegiance to it. This cult of the imagination as a sovereign and autonomous power became something like a religious faith:

where the imagination, the divine light, led, there, if he were to be true to his vocation of seer and prophet, the poet must follow. This conception was revolutionary; it would have been inconceivable to even the most "romantic" of earlier writers. For a fuller, and documented, treatment of this subject read the first chapter of Sir Maurice Bowra's *The Romantic Imagination.*

The second principle which all romanticists (again, in so far as they were romanticists) shared was *Individualism.* This was, of course, already implicit in the revolt against externally imposed rules and in the claim to individual liberty. But the implicit was made explicit and justified by philosophical doctrine. And this doctrine, though later modified in the light of experience, was provided in the first place by Rousseau and by his disciple Godwin. Both taught the perfectibility of man through (and this shows the danger of pigeon-holing) the rule of reason. To Rousseau and Godwin every man was potentially absolutely rational; all that was required was the removal of arbitrary external compulsion and reason alone would be sufficient to teach him to co-operate with his fellow men and to create a just society from which all evil would be banished. Rousseau believed that the result would be the formulation of good laws (expressing the General Will of rational beings); Godwin, whose *Political Justice* was, for a time, the bible of English romanticism, carried the doctrine to its logical conclusion, Anarchism, the abolition of all law and government, in the belief that only thus could each individual be set free to follow the light of his own reason, to the benefit of himself and of society. Disillusionment came, for most Godwinians, with the Terror. It was then that the second justification for individualism came into its own: the doctrine of the inner light of the imagination. Here again the authority lay within each individual and not with any external power.

And arising from this belief in the inner light came an extreme *subjectivity.* The classicist looks outwards for his truth: truth is the same for all men. But to the romantic truth lay within himself: what his imagination revealed to him must be accepted though all the world rejected it.

And from this individualism and subjectivity arose a fourth principle: *the reversal of the classical tenet "the general and not the particular"*. Blake wrote in the margin of Reynold's *Discourses*, "He who generalizes is an idiot". To the romanticist every human being was *unique*; the type was non-existent, a falsification to which no individual conforms. True, Wordsworth, Coleridge and, indeed, all the great romantics, believed that there were fundamental universal laws of human nature, but even so these could only be discovered in their individual, personal and often eccentric manifestations, by taking men one by one (as, in fact, Shakespeare had done), however much each one might differ from the norm. And to turn from literature to painting, compare a portrait by Ingres, with all the individuality ironed out, with one by the romanticist Géricault, with its concentration upon the personality of the sitter. There you have the difference between classicist generalization and romantic particularity.

A fifth principle: *Sensibility*. Wordsworth defined the poet as a man "with *more lively sensibility, more enthusiasm and tenderness* . . . than are supposed to be common among mankind". And you have only to read his poetry to discover his own capacity for passionate feeling. The Greeks believed in the Golden Mean, the middle way between too much passion and too little. To the romantics emotion tended to be good in itself; only in a state of heightened feeling, whether of pleasure or pain, was a man truly alive. And this with the great romantics, whose capacity for passionate feeling was in fact abnormally strong and who at the same time had enough of the classical element of restraint and rationality in their make-up to direct and discipline their passion, was a source of supreme strength. Their emotion never degenerated into emotionalism. But once "sensibility" became the fashion and everyone had to prove his worth by showing his capacity for feeling, then came the cult of emotion for emotion's sake, a whipping-up of small emotions into the semblance of big ones, a search for the sensational, however morbid, unwholesome or extravagant, which is one of the diseases of romanticism.

So much for the principles. It is when we come to their

expression in practice that the words "either . . . or" must be used. Here is a tabulated list of the sources from one or other of which the romantic imagination drew its inspiration:

(a) *Medievalism: the Gothic revival.* To the classicist of the eighteenth century the word "Gothic" was a pejorative; it meant "barbarous"; the Middle Ages were the Dark Ages. To the romanticist the Middle Ages became a world of enchantment, and "Gothic" stood for all the aspiration, the mystery, the spirituality and the wonder for which he craved. This idealization of the Middle Ages had various manifestations:

(1) The Gothic revival in architecture, beginning with Horace Walpole's Strawberry Hill and gathering impetus up to the end of the eighteenth century. In the full flood of the Romantic Movement Gothic became the only acceptable style of architecture.

(2) The use in narrative poetry of stories in a medieval setting, some (e.g. Coleridge's *Christabel* and Scott's narrative poems) inspired by the metrical romances, and others (e.g. Keats's *Isabella* and *The Eve of St. Agnes*) by tales of romantic love.

(3) In prose fiction the "Gothic romance", a fantastic tale of adventure, marvels and the supernatural in a Gothic setting, beginning with Horace Walpole's *The Castle of Otranto* and culminating in Mrs. Radcliffe. Then, still in the Gothic tradition but in reaction against the extravagance and irrational sensationalism of their precursors, Scott's medieval novels. And in France, in the Scott tradition, Victor Hugo and Chateaubriand.

(4) The rediscovery of ballads, beginning with Percy's *Reliques of Ancient English Poetry* and continued by Scott in his *Minstrelsy of the Scottish Border*. At the same time came the writing of poems modelled upon the ballads: *The Ancient Mariner* (the supreme work of genius among them), *La Belle Dame Sans Merci*, and innumerable others.

(5) The inflated reputation of Macpherson's *Ossian*. For what *Ossian* meant to the English romantics read the last paragraph of Hazlitt's *On Poetry in General*. But it was on the continent that its

evocation of a past barbarous, remote and mysterious became a major source of inspiration. It was translated into almost every European language. Goethe himself made one of the many German translations.

(6) The supernatural. The medieval romances were saturated in it, and so were many of the ballads. Here again, *The Ancient Mariner*, *Christabel* and *La Belle Dame Sans Merci*, and also *Lamia*. (This last, for all its deceptive Corinthian setting, was based on a Greek medieval, not classical, story.)

(b) *Geographical exploration:* an escape from the familiar, and hence prosaic, known world into the unknown, and hence mysterious, parts of the earth.

(1) Tales of voyages into the unknown: again *The Ancient Mariner* (it contains more of the elements of romance than, probably, any other single English poem). And, in French, *Paul et Virginie*. And Shelley's recurring image of the island, always a symbol of an unrealized ideal to attain which the poet must voyage over uncharted seas.

(2) Exoticism: especially the highly-coloured oriental exotic. *Kubla Khan* is far more than exotic, but its setting in Xanadu is essentially romantic. More typical are Byron's oriental tales.

(c) *Nature:* the escape from the city, gregarious, limited, sophisticated, man-made, known, to the infinite wonders of nature, unordered and untouched by man. And the more untamed and untamable by man the better. Hence *mountains*, which (incredible as this seems to us, who are still the heirs of the Romantic Movement) to the classicists of the eighteenth century had seemed the very type of the ugly, the barbarous. To almost every romantic mountains were the supreme symbol of sublime beauty, mystery, wonder, and of the divine. Read Shelley's *Mont Blanc*, Byron's *Manfred*, and—it goes without saying—Wordsworth's *Prelude*.

(d) *The primitive*. This stems from Rousseau's Noble Savage. He, and those who followed him in this belief, held that civilization destroys man's native innocence; it is unnatural; primitive man is spontaneous, his nature not repressed and deformed by social convention nor corrupted by worldliness. Read the passage in Wordsworth's Preface to *Lyrical Ballads* (the fifth paragraph) in which he defends his choice of "humble and rustic life" as the subject of his narrative poems. (Wordsworth's greatness was that he did not need to go to a fictitious "noble savage" for the simplicity and spontaneity he looked for; his human sympathy and insight revealed all that he wanted at his very door. Cf. the second paragraph of ch. XIV of *Biographia Literaria.*)

(e) *Utopianism:* the escape from the limitations of the imperfect present into a dream of a Golden Age of human perfectibility in an unknown—and unknowable—future: Shelley, *Prometheus Unbound.*

(f) *The macabre:* a product of the cult of emotionalism. Evil, death, the horrible, were dwelt upon in order to excite emotion. The schoolboy Shelley haunted grave-yards (*Hymn to Intellectual Beauty*); Mary Shelley wrote *Frankenstein*; Byron (alone among English poets, but the habit was widespread upon the continent) drank out of a skull.

(g) *Political liberty: republicanism.* Almost every romanticist, if he was interested in politics at all (and not all were) was, for a time at least, a republican. Rousseau began it with his doctrine of the General Will—and, of course, his extreme individualism and impatience with any restraint upon personal liberty. Then came the French Revolution, which, in its beginnings, seemed to the young idealists to usher in a heaven upon earth. (Read Wordsworth's *The French Revolution*, the poem beginning, "Oh! pleasant exercise of hope and joy!") And even when the Terror, and later Napoleon's dictatorship, brought disillusionment, the majority remained republican in principle: the French experiment had failed but the ideals of Liberty, Equality and Fraternity were still valid.

These are the main directions in which the romantic spirit set out to explore the mysteries, the wonders and the possibilities which lay beyond the classical "bounding line". The list is incomplete; I have omitted minor manifestations. Most of my examples are drawn from English literature, but the movement was international: the same elements will be found in the literature of any European country at the period.

One final point:

Classical versus Romantic

Of course we need both the classical and the romantic—the self-contained perfection of the Parthenon as well as the aspiring pinnacles of Chartres; Sophocles and Racine as well as Shakespeare; Homer and Milton as well as Wordsworth. Without either group we should be infinitely impoverished: a whole side of our nature would be starved. For human nature has two sides: the desire for order, wholeness and the repose of a rounded-off perfection, and the urge to adventure forth into the boundless. It is folly to pit the one against the other.

Nevertheless, each has the defects of its qualities and carries within itself the seeds of its own decay.

The danger which threatens the classical is a substitution of the letter for the spirit, a cult of rule for rule's sake, and a consequent *ossification.* In a great classical age the forms are still *flexible* and the classical restraint serves to discipline without inhibiting the imagination; the resultant works of art have a perfection, a serenity, a lucidity, unattainable by any romantic. But in all of these supreme creative imagination is there to be disciplined. The danger arises when the imagination flags. The forms remain to be imitated; their reproduction results in what *looks like* art. But they have become not a means to an end but an end in themselves, dead conventions, substitutes for the imaginative content which in the first instance they were created to embody. When this state of ossification has set in an imaginative artist, if he is not to be stifled, must break the mould and find new and unfamiliar forms in which to express himself.

Restraint can only make for living art when there is something to restrain. As Roy Campbell replied when certain novelists were praised for their "classical restraint":

You praise the firm restraint with which they write,
I'm with you there, of course:
They use the snaffle and the curb all right,
But where's the bloody horse?

With no imagination to be controlled all the controls in the world are useless: first find your horse, and then learn to ride him. That is what the late classicists forgot, and when the horse of the romantic imagination appeared it galloped in directions of which they had not conceived the possibility.

I have already suggested some of the diseases which threaten romanticism. The great romantics have explored realms which no classical writer would dare to enter and have infinitely extended the range of human sensibility. It is when we come to their lesser followers that the dangers are revealed: egotism, self-absorption and (for whoever looks solely at himself will discover that he is not as happy as he would like to be) self-pity; a pride in being different and at war with society; escapism—the creation of a dream world in which the hard facts of life are evaded; sentimentality; irrationality; sensationalism; a morbid obsession with the macabre. When these become the predominant mood the time has come for a swing of the pendulum back to classical rationality, objectivity and discipline.

A Note on Realism

The classical and the romantic are commonly represented as the two opposite poles towards one or other of which the arts inevitably gravitate. There is, however, a third possibility—realism: the representation of things as they are, with neither the classical ordering, formalizing and pattern-making, nor the romantic transcendentalism and search for a beyond. Flaubert set out to be a realist in this sense, and so did the Impressionist painters. Yet, in general, one may say that the majority of the so-called realists have in their interpretation of "reality" something of either the classical or of the romantic spirit: no novelist has confined himself more strictly to "things as they are" than did Jane Austen, and yet none is more classical, and, in painting, Hogarth, whom many would consider a realist *par excellence*, is classical in his composition. And, to take a far lesser novelist, H. G. Wells for all his realism was a romantic at heart with his dream of the redemption of the world by science. Nevertheless, one must allow for the possibility of this third alternative, the pure realist with nothing of either the classical or of the romantic in his make-up.

CHAPTER VII

THE NOVEL

THIS chapter presents a problem. Could I end my account of the novel at, roughly, the year 1920, all would be plain sailing. For, however much they may have differed in their choice of subject and their treatment of it, up to round about that date there was at least one thing about which all novelists (Sterne apart, but he stood alone*) were agreed: their business, whatever else they might do, was *to tell a story*. The story might contain many digressions; it might, or might not, take the form of a well-constructed plot; it might not be an end in itself but a means by which the writer communicated his philosophy of life; but story—a narrative of happenings following one another in chronological order and producing at least some degree of suspense as to "what happened next"—there must be, or the book was not a novel at all. This is true even of Proust (and he is half way to the modern novel): strip *A la Récherche du Temps Perdu* of its passages of psychological analysis, of its digressions into the philosophy of art, of its musical symbolism (of all, in fact, which makes it a very great novel), and the skeleton which would remain would be chronological narrative. If our novel reading stopped at this point all the novels which we had read (with the exception of *Tristram Shandy*) would be covered by some such definition as this: a fictitious prose narrative of some length, about possible people doing possible things in the real world, whose theme is human nature and human relationships. But then came James Joyce and Virginia Woolf. Though poles apart in every other respect, they had this in common: neither set out to "tell a story"; both for chronological narrative substituted something

* See Walter Allen, *The English Novel* (Pelican), pp. 76–80.

else. (What that "something else" was will come later.) We can still say that the theme of *Ulysses* and of Virginia Woolf's novels is human nature and human relationships as revealed in possible people living in the real world, but the word "narrative" must be omitted from the definition. And with the word must go all discussion of plot. Thus an *impasse*: either one omits "narrative" from the definition and plot from the amplification and so defines and amplifies something which the great novelists of the past would not have recognized as describing their works at all, or else one includes them and so excludes some of the most significant novels written within the last forty years.

The best solution of the problem, other than both in the definition and under the heading of Plot, a confusion of "either . . . ors", seems to be to divide this chapter into two sections, first the traditional novel, with all the characteristics which it shares in common with the modern, and then a postscript on the innovations which, following on from the experiments of James Joyce and Virginia Woolf, differentiate the modern from the old.

The Traditional Novel

The novel is a relatively recent phenomenon: *Don Quixote* has some, but not all, of the essential elements; the first fully-fledged novels did not appear until the early eighteenth century. In England it was Defoe who, with *Robinson Crusoe* and *Moll Flanders*, created the genre, and the earliest continental novels were roughly contemporary. *It was a new art form.*

And this new art form was born of the social conditions of the time. It arose in response to a demand by a new class of readers for a new kind of story. As far as we know, people have always wanted stories of some sort or another; from primitive myth and folk-lore, through, in Europe, the *Iliad*, the *Aeneid*, medieval romance, the *Decameron*, pastoral romance, right up to the present day, there has never been a time when the vast majority of people of all classes and kinds have not had an inexhaustible thirst (a) to live in imagination in the lives of others and (b) to be held in suspense as to "what happened next". And these are the marks of story: it gives vicarious experience and it holds our interest by alternately arousing our curiosity and satisfying it. The desire is universal; the only variations have consisted in the kinds of stories which people have wanted.

Now, up to round about the mid-seventeenth century the audience for stories was, with few exceptions, either simple and credulous—the common people—or else a leisured aristocracy or upper class. The former had their folk-tales and ballads, the latter either epics, sophisticated retellings of classical myths, romantic tales of chivalry or love, or highly literary pastoral fantasies, in all of which the humdrum workaday world held little place. They were a sheltered class, sheltered at least from the drudgery of working for their livings, and with leisure to indulge their fancies. But then, with the seventeenth century, came the rise to wealth and influence of the middle class, who had worked for their wealth, acquired it the hard way, and who knew that they must continue to work if they were to keep it—down-to-earth practical people with no nonsense about them. What use had they for noble knights rescuing lovely ladies from dragons or for fantastic shepherds writing sonnets when they should have been looking after their sheep? They knew that life was not like that; they did not believe a word of it nor did they want to. Yet, like everyone else they still did want to live in imagination in the lives of others and to enjoy the suspense of "what happened next".

Hence the novel: a story set in the world as practical realists knew it to be, peopled with men and women such as they saw around them and with happenings such as might occur any day to such people. That is the eighteenth-century novel, whether in England or on the Continent. And once the genre was created everyone read it—not only the middle class who had called it into being but the whole reading public. For another factor had intervened, the arrival of the Age of Reason; realism, not fantasy, is what reason demands. And even when the Romantic Movement produced the historical novel, with a setting far removed from everyday life, still the novelist set out to convince his readers that had they been there life would have been exactly as he describes it. In other words, the historical novel just as much as the one of contemporary life purports to be "a fictitious prose narration about possible people doing possible things in the real world".

Novels Bad, Good, and Great

Novel reading, quite literally, "takes us out of ourselves". Each of us, in our own persons, however eventful our lives, can have but one personality and one set of experiences; all the rest we can see only from the outside. When we read a novel, in proportion as it holds us, we escape from the restrictions of our own personalities and circumstances, and in imagination participate in those of the imaginary characters in the book; we live other lives besides our own. But whether this is a wholesome or a harmful occupation depends upon the novels that we read; if they are good ones it will lead to an enrichment, and if great to an immeasurable enrichment, of our whole personalities and sympathies, but if bad to nothing but debilitation. And this because in the one case we shall have escaped from ourselves into a wider and more varied reality, in the other into a world of make-believe and illusion.

The ultimate test of the quality of a novel lies, not in its "readability", essential though this is, nor in a well-constructed plot, nor in its literary style, but simply and solely in the degree of *truth* which it embodies, truth, first and foremost, in the characters themselves, then in the picture of the world in which they are placed, and, finally, in the novelist's sense of values, of what is, and what is not, worth living for.

Bad novels falsify; good novels are true *as far as they go*; each great novel is unique in that its author's genius has revealed to him some aspect of human nature which, but for him, would never have been known, and which, however many imitators he may have, can never be reproduced because it is embodied in characters which only he could have created. It has permanently extended humanity's awareness of itself.

To expand these statements:

Bad Novels

Leaving aside those novels which are bad simply from technical ineptitude (and they are almost certainly bad in other respects as well), the usual source of badness in a novel is *wish-fulfilment*. The bad novelist represents life not as it is, but as very probably he himself, and certainly the readers who he hopes will read his book, would like it to be. This wish-fulfilment may, on the part of the novelist, be quite unconscious; he may with the utmost sincerity be depicting life as he believes it to be, but nevertheless his own hidden wishes and illusions distort his vision and blind him to what he does not want to see. And, just because of this distortion, his book will, given sufficient technical skill, very probably be popular, possibly even a best-seller, for escape from the hard facts of everyday life into a world of illusion is what the majority of readers desire.

The degree of falsification in any given novel varies according to the motives of the writer, and to the public to whom the book is addressed. At the one end of the scale is the typical women's magazine story; this specimen—a short story, not a serial, but the principle is the same—is an actual example: poor dowdy little typist goes with glamorous friend to the Riviera; they meet a fabulously rich and devastatingly handsome young man; he of course falls for the glamorous friend; little typist goes out and buys a new dress and has a hair-do and beauty treatment; young man takes her out to dinner and proposes on the spot. The improbability here is self-evident, but what matters far more is its perverted values; marriage to wealth and good looks (and the girl does not know the man well enough to know whether he has anything else) is the highest goal to which feminine humanity can aspire, and all that is needed to attain to this state of bliss is a new dress and make-up. It is the ignorant plain girl's day-dream and could deceive no educated reader. And almost certainly the writer knew it; this kind of fantasy is purely commercial, written to sell.

But falsification can exist on a far more sophisticated level, and can be presented with a verisimilitude that may deceive all but the most discriminating readers. Here on the surface is complete realism; the characters appear to be the kind of people we know exist, and behave as such people would behave; the book may, very probably, contain "unpleasant" incidents and even have an unhappy ending, thus giving us the impression that we are facing the worst. Yet at its heart there will be a twist, and that in the direction of what the majority of people (its author almost certainly included) wish to believe: possessive passion is called love, or, conversely, selfless renunciation is too easily achieved; toughness and brutality may be represented as strength; the hero may be glamorized and, whatever venial faults he may for the sake of verisimilitude possess, too effortlessly good and noble to be true, or, if he is the contemporary "anti-hero", his faults are represented as "normal human nature" ("We are all like that if the truth were known; only the hypocrites pretend that they are not, so why should I, the reader, be ashamed if I am no better?"); tears may be too near the surface, and self-pity take the place of compassion; the characters' self-deceptions are represented as the truth. And all this is presented with such technical skill that, unless we are very much on the alert, we may be deceived into thinking that we are reading at least a good, if not a great, novel.

To this category belongs Galsworthy's *A Modern Comedy. The Forsyte Saga* is undoubtedly good, though even here there is a strain of falsity. (Read Max Beerbohm's parody of the early Galsworthy, *Endeavour*, in *A Christmas Garland*.) But *A Modern Comedy* is pure wish-fulfilment, though the wish-fulfilment of a sophisticated man of the world; the younger generation are sentimentalized: they are what an elderly man who prided himself on his "understanding", his "tolerance", wanted to believe (and knew that his readers wanted to believe), that the "shocking" young things of the 1920's were like at heart. So with Charles Morgan's too easy idealism; it evades too many problems; how nice it would be if things were as "beautiful" as he would have us believe! And so (though at his best he is outstandingly good) with Hemingway's occasional "soft-middles"; wherever, as it tends to do, his exaggerated cult of masculinity, violence and physical toughness conceals a soft core of sentimentality, an element of "badness" is there.

I have dealt only with the two extremes of falsity, the most naïve and the most sophisticated. The majority of popular novels lie somewhere between the two. You will, if you persevere, learn to recognize their falsity for yourselves.

Good Novels

I have said that good novels are true *as far as they go*. In so far as they are good (and even a good novel may have peripheral falsification; it is only falsity at the heart which makes for badness) nothing is falsified; people are like that; the characters are living people whose minds and emotions work as they would in real life; there are no short cuts to happiness; the chain of factual and moral cause and effect works out with no evasions. And the values are sound: our sympathies are engaged on the side of goodness, generosity, compassion; meanness and self-seeking are exposed as what they are; however much we may sympathize with, or even feel affection for, "bad" characters we are never left in doubt that their faults are faults, even though pardonable ones. But there is a point beyond which the novelist cannot go; he gives us nothing which, even though it may be new to us, is not already a part of the current coin of humanity's awareness of itself. He may (and almost certainly does) break new ground in his choice of situation, presenting old truths in a new and contemporary setting, and setting his characters modern problems to deal with which would have been unthinkable to his predecessors. But all the time his insight goes no deeper than has that of other good novelists in the past; in so far as it goes deeper, as, possibly, does Graham Greene's in his sense of a spark of divine goodness even in the depths of evil, he is at least on the border-line between the good and the great. Good novels are very well worth reading; they do not mislead us (except in so far as we may be led to believe that they contain the whole truth), and they extend our imaginative range and our sympathies far beyond the limits of our personal experience. But always there is something lacking, a level of truth to which the book does not penetrate.

The Great Novel

I have said that each great novel is unique in that its author's genius has embodied in living characters some truth about human nature and the human condition of which humanity but for him would have been unaware. Of the good novel we say, "Yes, how true!", but of the great, "So *that* is the truth!" And this equally of Jane Austen's razor-fine dissection of petty vanities and self-deceptions and of Dostoevsky's creation of the hell upon earth of a murderer's mind. And this not only of what people are, but of the values by which they live. The rule of thumb code of conventional morality is seen as the clumsy instrument which in fact it is. Good remains good, evil evil—in fact black may become blacker, white whiter, goodness be shown to have a beauty which we had not suspected and the sheer horror of evil laid bare to us for the first time. But always there will have been some shift in values—a realization that good and evil, wisdom and folly, are not always to be found where we would expect to look for them—and this shift always in the direction of a deeper truth.

What we ask of the great novelist is that, however much else he may or may not be able to do, he shall at least in some one direction have this unique vision. Balzac has it in his perception of the corrupting power of money, Emily Brontë in her poet's insight into the oneness of the primitive human passions and the elemental forces of nature; Tolstoy, in *Anna Karenina*, in his penetration into the meaning of marriage (remember that there are two contrasted marriages in the book, not only Anna's), and in *War and Peace* into the interactions in a whole nation at war of the lives of individuals and of history; Dickens in his eye for the grotesque, both humorous and terrifying, and, in all but his earliest novels, in his boding sense of the sinister; Scott (in his great Scottish novels) in his power of recreating the past of his own country in terms of the religious fanaticism of individuals and sects; Herman Melville, in *Moby Dick*, in his transcendent vision of man pitted against the non-human forces of nature symbolized by the white whale. And so of all the rest. And, the giants apart, wherever even a lesser novelist has this unique vision he has, to that extent, an element of greatness. So Conrad: his range (except in his greatest and most complex novel, *Nostromo*) is narrow; his recurring theme is that of human courage and endurance tested to the uttermost, but where he treats of this successfully, as he does in *The Shadow Line*, he stands alone. And D. H. Lawrence: he is a faulty, and at his worst a bad, writer, but his mystical conception of the nature of human relationships and of the life-destroying power of a mechanized society (for this, and not, as is commonly supposed, sex, is his gospel) has this uniqueness. Whereas Trollope, for all his genius for creating living characters, just misses greatness, for his values are trite, the common coin of the average man.

And, where this unique vision is present, faults which would damn a lesser writer are irrelevant to the question of greatness. The giant may be flawed, but he is a giant nonetheless. Dickens can lapse into sickly sentimentality and his drama may become melodrama; we may wish it were otherwise, but his positive achievement lies elsewhere. Scott's lovers are stuffed with sawdust, but we ignore them; it is not for the love-interest that we read him. Charlotte Brontë's Rochester is fantasy, but he takes nothing from the truth of the passionate and love-starved Jane Eyre. The ideal would, of course, be that all novelists should imitate Jane Austen and attempt nothing that they cannot do.

But where they do not we must take them as they are, read them for what they uniquely can give us, and put up as best we can with the rest. The alternative is to miss some of the supreme experiences which novel reading can give us.

Character

The power to create living characters is the novelist's essential gift. For not only do we read novels for the pleasure and emotional release of living in the lives of people other than ourselves, and not only does whatever truth the novel may contain come to us embodied in these living people or not at all, but it is only in virtue of his imaginative power to create such characters that the novelist himself comes to know the truth about them. And this is so even where, as it was with Henry James, his starting point is some particular moral or psychological situation which he wishes to explore; he may have a general idea, based on his observation of life, of what he expects to find, but it is only as the characters take on flesh and blood in his imagination that understanding becomes possible. And this implies that his characters must be not merely life-*like* but *alive*. And there is a world of difference between the two.

Characters Life-Like and Living

In the worst novels the characters are not even like life; any intelligent reader knows at once that people do not behave like that. These we can dismiss without further discussion; no one who reads this book is likely to be deceived by them. The characters which may lead us astray and deceive us into thinking that we are reading a good, or even a great, novel, are those which are *like* life and which yet are not living. By a life-like character I mean one who, thanks to his maker's observation of the surface of human behaviour and to his technical skill (which may be very great), goes through all the motions appropriate to a living person of his type, says the right things in the idiom we should expect of his class or situation in life, thinks, up to a point, the right thoughts, registers the right emotions, weeps when tears are demanded (or, if it is more in character, shows a stiff upper lip), laughs when he should laugh, shows all the expected symptoms of fear, anger, joy, hope, despair, *but all this is imposed upon him from without by the conscious choice of his maker; he has no inside.* He is a puppet dancing on a string at the will of a highly skilful puppet-master; his verisimilitude is external; he has no inner core of life in himself from which his behaviour inevitably but incalculably springs. He does, thinks and feels what any of us would expect such a person to do, think and feel, or, if he should spring surprises upon us, these surprises are clearly calculated and engineered by his manipulator and are well within the bounds of what we may be expected to accept.

A living character, on the other hand, has such an inner core. The novelist's imagination has worked *from within outwards*, not manufacturing a life-like puppet, but creating an inner living self, out of which behaviour, thought, feeling, action can be trusted to emerge. And once the living being is created nothing can be imposed upon it from without, or if for the sake of the exigencies of the plot the novelist does (as does Thackeray with Becky Sharp) so impose his will, we at once notice that the life has gone out of the creation; it has become a puppet. The living character is an integrated organism obeying, not his maker, but the laws of his own being. And should he behave unexpectedly his behaviour is not "out of character" but only goes to show that, as with all living beings, there is more to him than we, or possibly even his creator when he first conceived him, suspected. Nearly all Jane Austen's characters are, in this sense, living; so are Scott's Scottish characters (but not, of course, whatever their nationality, his lovers); all of Tolstoy's; Jane Eyre; most of Hardy's country people; Dickens's major grotesques and scoundrels (his "good" characters are inclined to be puppets and many of his minor "comics" are mere figures of fun); Dostoevsky's supremely; Balzac's major characters; Madame Bovary; Joyce's

Leopold Bloom; in fact, all the characters in virtue of whom the great novelists have earned their title.

Anyone who has read E. M. Forster's *Aspects of the Novel* will recognize that my distinction between "life-like" and "living" characters largely corresponds with (and is in fact partly borrowed from) his between flat characters and characters in the round. The main difference lies in the placing of Dickens: in my classification his (best) characters are "living", in E. M. Forster's "flat". And, valid as the "flat/round" distinction is in the case of the majority of novelists, I find it impossible to accept as the ultimate test one which places Dickens on the wrong side of the line. Either Dickens's characters are not flat (and it is true that E. M. Forster weights the scales unfairly against him by taking as his example the very minor Mrs. Micawber, instead of, as he might, one of his major and fully developed characters) or else "roundness", as E. M. Forster defines it, though a quality of almost all the best characters in fiction, cannot be the last word. Very briefly, a flat character is two-dimensional: there is nothing to it except the side which the novelist shows us; a round one is three-dimensional: we could walk round it and see for ourselves all that the novelist has not told us. It is true that (except perhaps in the case of Jasper in *Edwin Drood*) Dickens's characters do exist only in what he shows us of them, but nevertheless what he does show us comes from inside themselves; background characters and failures apart, each has a living core within him, an abounding life which is not, as E. M. Forster suggests, a projection of Dickens's self, but is his own. He does what he does because he is what he is; once created he "could no other", and thus, even though he may be "flat" in E. M. Forster's sense of the word, he is, as I use the terms, not "life-like" but "alive". Nevertheless, the "flat/round" distinction is a valuable one.

And this leads to a further distinction, a subdivision within the category of "living" characters: *the individual and the type*. It is, in general, by their power of individualization that we appraise the great novelists. To Jane Austen there is no such thing as "a" snob; there are snobs and snobs, no two alike, and her genius lies in the subtlety with which she distinguishes between them. So with Fielding: Tom Jones is not "a" young man of a certain type; he is Tom Jones himself, with much in common with, but quite as much which differentiates him from, other young men of his kind. So Trollope: Mrs. Proudie is Mrs. Proudie, and no one else. (Were creativeness alone, without perception of values, enough to make a great novelist Trollope would rank not very far below the greatest.) So George Eliot, in her women at least. (Her weak young men tend to be variations on a theme.) So Defoe: Moll Flanders is Moll Flanders, and could be no one else. And so of the majority of the great novelists. But human beings possess not only differences but resemblances, and it may happen, though it rarely does, that a novelist may concentrate so entirely upon certain fundamental passions which his characters share in common with others of their type that he is little concerned with what is peculiar to themselves, and yet create a character who, though simplified, is intensely alive. All Hardy's tragic heroines are but variations of the same woman: the essentially feminine whose whole personality is centred upon the passionate desire to fulfil herself in self-giving love, and who is thus the predestined victim of a man unworthy of her. Hardy is not concerned with what differentiates one such young woman from another; he is content to treat again and again the same tragic theme, varying only the situation and more superficial details. But the living core of passion is there; the characters are alive.

Plot

It is here that we come to the parting of the ways between the traditional and the modern novel; both equally demand that truth to human nature, human relationships and values should be embodied in living characters, but it is only in the traditional novel that we look for a plot. But granted, as the traditional novel assumes, that it is the business of the novelist to tell a good story, then, other things being equal (and, as you will see as we proceed, they are not always equal; some of the best narrative novels are nearly plotless), it is generally agreed that the best way to tell a story is to turn it into a plot.

For story and plot are not the same thing. The difference between the two is thus defined by E. M. Forster: "We have defined a story as a narrative of events arranged in their time-sequence. A plot is also a narrative of events, *the emphasis falling on causality*." He then goes on to reduce each to a one sentence formula: " 'The king died and *then* the queen died' is a story. 'The king died and then the queen died *of grief*' is a plot." (*Aspects of the Novel*, p. 16; italics mine.) In the first, for all that we are told, it was mere chance that the king died before the queen and not after her, or that the queen died at all. In the second there is, by implication, a therefore; the order of events could not be reversed, for the queen's death was caused by the king's. *Story proceeds by a series of "thens", plot by a series of "therefores"*. And the more faultless is the chain of "therefores" the more perfect, technically, is the plot. Ideally when we reach the end of a traditional novel we should be able to look back and see that had one single incident been different the conclusion would not have worked out as it has. Whereas story holds us in irrational suspense—anything may happen—in plot the suspense becomes rational; we see not only what happens, but why. A pattern emerges; life becomes understandable, not a thing of bits and pieces and loose ends, but a logical progression towards an end.

This of the perfect plot, when it is the work of a genius who is its master and not its slave. Nothing, granted that a story is to be told, can give us greater aesthetic satisfaction: by the end everything is rounded off into a meaningful unity, and yet never for a moment has "life" been sacrificed to art. But such perfection is very rare, and where we have to choose between "life" with loose-ends and a straight-jacket of plot which forces an artificial pattern of behaviour upon living characters, then loose-ends and "life" win every time. And most novelists have to make the choice. For to write a novel in which the plot is technically faultless and which yet leaves the characters free to be themselves, as living beings must be free, demands a very special kind of genius, the gift of conceiving of plot and character in one creative act—characters who would in the situation in which they are placed inevitably do what the plot demands, and a plot which is a series of "therefores" which are exactly what those characters would bring about. Jane Austen has it to perfection; so, though perhaps less infallibly, has Henry James; Flaubert in *Madame Bovary*. And George Eliot in *Middlemarch*; she never pulls strings and yet everything works out to its inevitable conclusion.

But when the plot is artificially imposed upon the characters from without, then we can only wish it away; far better a loosely connected series of "thens" in which the characters are free to be themselves and to work out their own destinies than that their creator should visibly be seen to intervene in order to work up to a predetermined end. Take *Moll Flanders*; it is still in the main in the plotless picaresque* tradition out of which the novel as we know it was born—a series of adventures and misfortunes, one succeeding another by chance rather than by causality. And yet there is not, until we approach the end, one incident which does not help to build up and to enrich Moll's self and make her one of the most living characters in fiction. But unfortunately Defoe believed that a tidy ending was necessary, and the coincidences by which he achieves his "dramatic" conclusion strain credulity to breaking point. So with Fielding. In *Tom Jones*, it is true, he needed to pull no strings; his plot, complex as it is, is the logical outcome of what his characters are and of the situation in which he has placed them. But when we come to *Amelia* the whole virtue of the book lies in the picaresque series of "thens" by which we get to know Amelia herself, her Billy and the world in which they live; the manipulation of coincidence by which the "happy ending" is achieved is so forced as to be ludicrous. So, often,

* From the Spanish *picaro*, a rogue. The original picaresque novel told the story of the adventures of a vagabond who set out on a journey upon which anything might happen to him; it was all "thens" and no "therefores". Later the "rogue" element dropped out; the series of unrelated but entertaining adventures remained; *The Pickwick Papers* is pure picaresque in this "rogueless" form.

with Dickens; in *Bleak House* the plot is organic, but elsewhere—in old Martin's play-acting, at the end of *Martin Chuzzlewit* and in Mr. Boffin's comparable deception in *Our Mutual Friend*—the characters themselves are falsified, a far worse fault than the resort to coincidence. And even in Hardy the unhappy coincidences which seal the fate of his tragic victims are too evidently the work of Hardy himself and make it only too clear that the plot has been devised not, as he would have us believe, by an evil destiny but by the author.

All these novelists—even, though to a limited extent, Hardy—were, however, writing in a relatively primitive convention, a convention based upon the false assumption that the day-to-day chain of cause and effect would not in itself be sufficient to hold the reader's interest without the added inducement of a mystery to be solved or an apparently insuperable obstacle to be removed or, perhaps, the expectation of a dramatic reversal of fortune in the last chapter. Jane Austen, of course, had known better; we know that she is keeping no secrets from us (or if, as in the case of Jane Fairfax's engagement to Frank Churchill, she does keep one, it makes not the slightest difference to our interest if we guess it), and so we are content to watch how one thing leads on to another without hurrying on to the end to discover what card she has hidden up her sleeve. But she stood alone; in England at least the final break came only with George Eliot's rational faith in her readers' adult intelligence and in their willingness to read on without the carrot of a "surprise ending" dangling in front of their noses.* The gain was immense, as one recognizes if one compares any of the great novels written in the latter half of the nineteenth century with those in the old convention; the interest is no longer divided; we are free to concentrate on the true theme of the novel, human nature, human behaviour and psychological and moral cause and effect, without the distraction of an irrelevant puzzle element. Look for instance, from this point of view,

* Cf. Lord David Cecil's chapter on George Eliot in his *Early Victorian Novelists*. And for Hardy's failure completely to break with the old "dramatic" convention, his *Hardy the Novelist*.

at *The Brothers Karamazov*; plot is there in the sense of causality; the situation at the beginning inevitably works itself out to the destined conclusion; yet it is so unobtrusive that we are hardly aware of its presence; we are participating, not in a manipulated story, but in life, as from day to day one thing succeeds another until the end is reached. So with Tolstoy, Flaubert, Henry James, Proust—all the great who wrote once the bad old convention was outmoded.

Yet even so, except in these greatest, a certain sense of manipulation, of contrivance, tended to remain—a too great awareness on the part of the reader that, even though he is keeping no secrets, the novelist knew in advance the end to which all his "therefores" must lead, that the characters were not quite free agents but were being directed by their maker towards a predetermined conclusion, that everything was going to be tidied up at the end as things never are in life, that life itself was being subordinated to construction. So the time came when the question was asked, "Why have a plot at all? Why not discard this business of 'what happened next and what came of it?' in favour of the true theme of the novel, 'What are human beings like in themselves?' " Hence the Modern Novel.

But before we come to the Modern Novel there is one more point to discuss:

Different Levels of Truth in the Novel: Realism and its Reverse

The first essential for a novel is that it must be true to life. But to "life" in what sense? A photograph is "true" in that it shows what its subject *looks like*, yet what a very different truth it tells us from, say, a portrait by Rembrandt. The one shows the recognizable surface appearance, what we could all see for ourselves; the other the inner being which was visible only to the imaginative intuition of an artist of genius. And it is, of course, with this deeper level of truth that the novel is concerned.

But this is not to say that accuracy in the representation of externals—realism, as it is called—has no place in the novel; after all, Rembrandt did not plunge straight to the depths and attempt to portray a disembodied soul; the surface, the appearance, is there, and it is probably represented with accuracy, however the spirit may shine through. So with the novel: while a photographically-exact representation of human behaviour and environment which is that and nothing more can, however deceptively "life-like" it may appear to be, tell us nothing of what it is the novelist's business to reveal—in fact, can only falsify by suggesting that this is all that there is to tell or even blind us to actual falsification of what it is suggested lies beneath the surface—nevertheless it is often only by the accuracy of his observation of the surface details of everyday life—of the houses people live in, the work they do, the food they eat, their manner of speech—that he can approach what lies beneath.

Whether the novelist should be a realist or the reverse depends upon the nature of his theme. Where realism is required is, primarily, in the social novel. And by the social novel I mean one whose theme is the interrelations of men and women belonging to a distinctive social group who, however individual each may be in himself, are to a greater or lesser extent in their behaviour conditioned by, and show what they are by their response to, the conventions, the material circumstances, the opportunities or limitations, of that group. Here if the inner life is not to be falsified the settings which condition it must be represented with absolute accuracy, even, probably, down to the minutest details. Take Jane Austen: her theme is, it is true, human wisdom and folly, moral integrity and the lack of it, but the tests to which her characters are subjected are all set by the particular social convention into which they were born, the convention of the English country gentry of the early nineteenth century; it is in relation to this convention, with its class distinctions, its code of manners, of decorum, its dependence upon a certain level of income, that they show what they are; the moral problems may be major ones, but the form in which they present themselves is always a choice between one or other course of action within this social framework. And it is by the absolute exactitude with which Jane Austen represents this framework—the slight variations of idiom or of manners which distinguish the gentleman from the not-quite-gentleman, the errors of taste which betray vulgarity, not so much of birth as of nature, the things to which pretentiousness pretends, the exact degree of social deprivation caused by an inadequate income, and all the rest—that she gives such absolute validity to the moral choices of her characters. And, to take a very different example, *Madame Bovary*: given her temperament, it was the specific limitations and frustrations of the society into which she had the misfortune to be born—the society of French provincial life—which made her what she was; it is the cumulative effect of a series of *little* things—often sordid little things—that builds up to her tragedy, and it is by the meticulous accuracy with which Flaubert represents them that we feel their impact upon her. Here again, the theme is not a human being as she is in herself, but a human being as she becomes in relation to a given social pattern; omit the environment, or blur it, and there would be nothing left for her to re-act to. In such novels realism—absolute accuracy in the representation of everyday life—is essential.

But at the other end of the scale is the novel whose theme is not the individual as a member of a specific social group, but those elements in the individual which are purely personal to himself, and his relationship, not to society as a whole, but to some other individual, or individuals, as separate as himself. Here the novelist can by-pass realism and plunge straight to the depths. The characters must of course be placed in a world sufficiently resembling the real one to give them a credible field of action, but granted sure enough insight into their inner being their creator can safely ignore any external detail which is not relevant to his theme. In *Wuthering Heights* Emily Brontë is not concerned with the everyday life of a typical Yorkshire farming community, made up of the day-to-day routine of work, of eating and drinking, of neighbourliness, of all the little things which condition the pattern of human relationships in such a community; her theme is Heathcliff and Catherine in isolation, in relation only to each other in the solitude of the Yorkshire moors. It is the forces of nature which are their environment, and the evocation of these alone is essential to her poetic purpose. So with a lesser book, but one nearly faultless in its way, Alain-Fournier's *Le Grand Meaulnes*. Here critics have pointed out minor errors of verisimilitude; no French school could be run on the lines of the one which is the setting of the main part of the story, nor is the fancy-dress party entirely credible on the realistic level. But given the book's theme, the poetic evocation of tragic adolescent love, such improbabilities are irrelevant; we do not notice them, for it is not in relation to school or to the social conventions of the great house where the party takes place that the schoolboy lover reveals what he is, but solely in his experience of romantic love. So with Kafka's *The Castle*; here the happenings are not merely improbable but frankly impossible, but the theme is not how, on the level of actuality, a corrupt bureaucracy functions, but the nightmare horror of the helplessness of the individual caught up in such an impersonal and mindless tyranny.

To sum up: the level on which a novel must be true is the deeper one of human emotion, motive and values. Surface realism is only essential where the theme is one in which what the characters are is conditioned by the minor details of their social environment; where they are not so conditioned, surface inaccuracies, or even distortions, can be accepted or ignored.

The Modern Novel

The majority of novels written today are no more "modern" than are those which were written fifty years ago. For when we use the word "modern" in this context we are indicating not the date at which any given novel was written but the kind of novel which it is—a kind which (the freak *Tristram Shandy* apart) could not have been written before the 1920's, in which decade were published James Joyce's *Ulysses* and Virginia Woolf's *Mrs.*

Dalloway and *To the Lighthouse*. A contemporary novel which sets out first and foremost to entertain us by "telling a good story" in the old way is no more a modern novel than are a neo-Gothic church or a "Stockbroker's Tudor" villa modern architecture; a novel is only modern, as distinct from contemporary, if either, in imitation of Joyce and Virginia Woolf, it rejects direct chronological narrative completely in favour of something else, or if, even though it does tell a story, as a result of the experiments which followed their questioning of the traditional novel form, it tells it with a difference.

The Stream of Consciousness

I have said in the previous paragraph that James Joyce and Virginia Woolf rejected chronological narrative in favour of "something else". That "something else" was a technique known as the Stream of Consciousness. The method was, it is true, not their own discovery; it had already been used by a minor novelist, Dorothy Richardson. But it was its use by these two major writers which showed its possibilities as a way of exploring human personality without what had come to many people to seem to be the falsification of experience inevitable if human behaviour was forced into the pattern of "a well-constructed plot", and which marks the turning point in the evolution of the Modern Novel.

No two writers could be more different in every other respect than the essentially masculine, muscular, and metaphysical genius of James Joyce and the fastidious, feminine sensibility of Virginia Woolf, but they had this one thing in common: both by introspection had discovered that the inner workings of the human mind, its motives, its awareness, follow a course of their own, set in motion, it is true, by, but once set in motion having a sequence and logic totally different from, the external happenings which follow one another in chronological order. And to both it was clear that it was this *inner* series of "therefores" and not the external "therefores" of "what *happened* next and what came of it?" that condition both what we are and our relations to other people. Whereas the traditional novel had worked from without inwards, showing what people are through what they do and through their reaction to an ordered series of events, Joyce and Virginia Woolf reversed the process: they started from the inside, from the awareness of their characters, and showed external happenings only as, and in the order that, they impinged upon, and set in motion a train of associations in, the consciousness of the character himself. Both saw the novelist's task not as the planning of a series of happenings progressing towards a predetermined end, but as the watching of the moment to moment changes within the consciousness of a person to whom the future was totally unknown, and thus the discovery, and transmission to the imagination of his readers, of what life in fact is in the process of living it, and not what it seems to be to a story-teller who, knowing the end, can be wise after the event.

And their method was, once having (the first requirement in any novelist, traditional or modern) created a living character, *to allow us, without the intervention of a narrator, to eavesdrop upon that character's "stream of consciousness"*, to overhear for ourselves all that passes through his mind, with all the irrationality, the inconsequence, the illogical association of ideas, the leaps from one topic to another, from present to past and back again, which introspection tells us is how our minds in fact do work and which, far more than logical thought and rational decision, both reveal what in the depths we are, the emotional sources of our responses, and condition our behaviour. Selection of course is there: the novel is art and not nature; the character remembers what it suits his creator's purpose that he should remember; the switches are not fortuitous. But the impression which we are intended to receive is that we are catching a human mind off its guard and not being told about, but ourselves watching, the processes by which it works.

When the technique is used in its pure form, as it is with questionable success in Virginia Woolf's *The Waves* and with supreme mastery in the last great chapter of *Ulysses*, there is no intervention by a narrator at all: all we know of the situation, the setting, the relationships, of who's who and what's what, and of the time sequence, we must deduce for ourselves from what we overhear passing through the thoughts of the characters. More usually, however, the "stream of consciousness" is combined with a greater or less amount of direct narration; the novelist in his own person sets the scene, introduces the characters and provides the essential narrative links between one situation and another, allowing the eavesdropping to begin only when we know who is who and the situation to which any given character is reacting. This is the method of Virginia Woolf's *To the Lighthouse*. Here the book opens with a situation: a group of people are brought together as hosts and guests in a house on the coast of Scotland; a picnic at a lighthouse has been planned; it is only when the scene is set that the true theme of the book emerges: not a series of happenings but the psychological and emotional changes in each member of the group, and the shifts in the relationships between them which, in the course of one day, this bringing together, and first the expectation, and then the cancellation, of the expedition, set in train. It is only for these changes and shifts that the stream of consciousness technique is used. But if the fact that the book contains a certain modicum of direct narrative should mislead us into reading it as a "story", not only shall we be disappointed but we shall miss the whole point.

In the case of James Joyce, the major genius of the two, it is true that the stream of consciousness was only one of his technical innovations; in *Ulysses* he uses symbolic action, surrealist fantasy, an associative manipulation of language—almost anything, in fact, except straight old-fashioned story telling—to create a pattern of interrelated themes. Yet even here it is mainly through his use of the stream of consciousness that, working from the inside, he builds up his Leopold Bloom, one of the most living characters in fiction, and, in the short run at least, it was the new inwardness made possible by his and Virginia Woolf's use of the technique that revolutionized the whole conception of the novel form, not only in the English-speaking world but on the continent.

The Novel since Joyce and Virginia Woolf

The distinguishing mark of the novel in the last forty or so years is, as I have said, that either it follows James Joyce and Virginia Woolf in the use of the stream of consciousness technique, or, if it should "tell a story", as a result of their questioning of the whole conception of what a novel should be it tells it with a difference. And this difference, whatever else it may be—and the experiments in new ways of "telling a story" have been innumerable—is always in the direction of inwardness, of, even when the narrative is chronological, using "happenings" rather to reveal the pattern of emotional and psychological "therefores" which actuate the characters than to use the characters to bring a series of happenings to a required conclusion.

In the English language—he was of course American—probably, despite his faults, the experimenter who comes nearest to greatness has been William Faulkner. His *The Sound and the Fury* is pure stream of consciousness, going further in the direction of apparent inconsequence than any other writer would have dared, for it is the consciousness of an idiot who confuses past and present, one generation with another, and yet through whose confused and distorted "rememberings" we are able to reconstruct the evil story of his family through two generations, and who, just because he is an idiot, adds the final touch of nightmare futility which Faulkner desired:

> It [life] is a tale
> Told by an idiot, full of sound and fury,
> Signifying nothing.

Many of his novels, however, including his late trilogy, *The Village*, *The Town* and *The Mansion*, are narrated. But they are narrated in a new way, or rather in a variety of new ways; in the trilogy the narrative is shared out between various characters; none knows the whole truth; each one's version tells us more about himself than about the facts of the case; it is left to us to deduce these facts. And though the three books do add up to a story of a kind—the rise and ultimate fall of the outrageous

Snopes family and their impact upon a whole community—of plot in the formal sense there is none; themes emerge, disappear, re-emerge, although every thread leads back to the Snopeses.

Then—another great writer—there is Camus. For all its narrative form, if we read *La Peste* as a story of an actual plague in the city of Oran, it leaves us merely puzzled—things do not happen like that. But the plague is a symbolic plague; it is in the symbolism that the meaning lies. And Sartre's *La Nausée*; of "story" there is none; all that "happens" is the disintegration of the world of appearances as seen subjectively through the eyes of the "hero"; it is the expression in novel form of Sartre's Existentialist philosophy; if we read it as a narrative of objective happenings it is meaningless.

And Musil's *Der Mann ohne Eigenschaften* (*The Man Without Qualities*): it is narrative; it has a beginning and a middle and, had the author lived to complete the last volume, it would undoubtedly have had an end. But of plot, in the traditional sense, there is none; throughout the two completed volumes, though "the man without qualities" himself remains a constant, characters come and go, themes appear, are dropped, and reappear; when we expect to be told "what happened next" very probably nothing happens—the scene is changed and our question remains unanswered. To read it as straight "story" is impossible; its structure, development, meaning, are to be found not in the "therefore . . . therefore" of a sequence of events, but in the shifting relationship of a group of intensely, sometimes fantastically, "living" characters and in a pattern of recurring symbols.

These novels, and others of their kind, are (with the exception, perhaps, of *La Nausée*, whose significance is philosophical rather than artistic) *as works of the creative imagination* among the most exciting of contemporary writings; they have extended the range of our imaginative awareness of ourselves and of the nature of human experience. The trouble is that with them the novel has ceased to be what in its origins it set out to be, a form of entertainment. All are difficult books; all must be read with intense concentration, and, it may be, read and re-read, if we are to piece together for ourselves the allusions, the symbolic significances, the psychological and emotional juxtapositions by which the effect is achieved. They can give us intense pleasure, but we must work for our pleasure; there is no sitting back and reading on effortlessly from page to page and absorbing the "meaning" almost unconsciously as we go. And that—to extend our imaginative experience and our knowledge of life while we thought that we were being merely entertained by "story-telling"—was what the novel form was evolved to do. It used our inborn love of story in order to give us something else.

So the question: although no one would wish the "difficult" novel away as a form of imaginative literature, is it not possible to restore the entertainment value of the novel while retaining something of the inwardness, the immediacy and the freedom from the rigidity of plot which the "difficult" novel has given us? Hence the experiments in "story, but story with a difference".

At the end of an already overlong chapter it is impossible to enumerate more than a few—perhaps arbitrarily selected—of the more interesting of the writers of "story with a difference". Henry Green is one of them; in his *Loving* he is seemingly giving us a simple and straightforward love story, ending, almost unbelievably in a modern novel, "and they lived happily ever after". But the significance of the book lies in its poetic overtones, in its evocative symbolism; if we miss these we have missed its whole mood. In *Caught*, on the other hand, there is no continuous narrative; by placing his characters in a series of discontinuous *situations* (during the air raids of the last war) he allows them to reveal themselves and their relationships. And a pure novel of situation is his *Party Going*: a group of smart Mayfair—or near-Mayfair—young things are setting out for the Riviera; they are held up by fog at Victoria; they take refuge in the hotel and, against a background of (symbolic) community singing by the crowd of suburban commuters outside, *they talk*. That is all, but through their often brainless chatter by the time the fog lifts we know them far better than they know themselves.

Then there is Anthony Powell's still (in 1964) unfinished *roman fleuve*, *The Music of Time*. Here volume follows volume, each self-contained in itself, but each part of a larger whole; the narration is quite orthodox, but in the place of plot is an ever widening network of relationships, the theme being the changes wrought by time; a group of young (and in the later volumes not so young) men, whom we have first met as schoolboys, part, meet again by chance, and are again scattered and re-united, each having meantime collected round him a new circle of acquaintances; the several groups intermix and establish new relationships in a more and more complex pattern. Design is there, but of plot there is none; it is impossible to believe that when the last volume appears we shall discover that the innumerable threads were ever intended to be neatly tied up, and we do not wish them to be.

And there is Ivy Compton-Burnett's use of dialogue almost to the exclusion of narration, with its sense of immediacy: we have the experience not of being *told about* the happenings by an intruding intermediary, but of being ourselves present, in first-hand contact with the speakers whose conversation we are overhearing and who, no more than ourselves, know what it is all leading up to.

These three unmistakably break with tradition. But even in those novels which most of us read as straight story-telling the new experiments have made their impact. Compare anything of Graham Greene's with a novel of fifty years ago. The plot is far freer, less contrived; dialogue will probably predominate over narrative; many chronological links will be omitted: instead of, as in the older novels, being told the events which led from one situation to another we shall, on beginning a new chapter, be plunged directly into a new situation and be left to discover from their talk the essentials of how the speakers got there. And always, however sensational the happenings may be, they are there not primarily for the sake of plot, but to enable the characters to show what they are in themselves.

Conclusion

Many modern novels are, as I have said, difficult. Why, then, read them? Why not be content to be entertained by the straight story-telling which all the great novelists of the past found served their purpose? The answer is simple: whereas in the past story-telling and genius went together, today in many cases we have to choose between one and the other; whether we like it or not, the most gifted of contemporary and near-contemporary novelists have, with few exceptions, been experimenters; if we confine our reading to straight story-telling we shall either find relatively little to read, or else be obliged to fall back upon the second-rate. And meantime, for want of the effort required to overcome difficulties, we shall have missed much of the most significant and imaginatively exciting writing of the last half-century. The pleasures of the modern novel may have to be worked for, but the work will be amply rewarded.

CHAPTER VIII

NOTES ON ARISTOTLE'S *POETICS*

ARISTOTLE'S *Poetics* is a difficult book for several reasons:

(a) The Greek habit of thought is often remote from ours, and, if we are unfamiliar with it, it is difficult to follow. This is true of all Greek philosophy, but:

(b) The *Poetics* is written in note form; it is the notes of lectures which Aristotle gave to Athenian students. Hence grammatical links are often missing in the original.

(c) Even these notes are incomplete: tragedy is dealt with in full, comedy and epic are only touched upon in passing; the full treatment of these and the sections dealing with the other classes of poetry are lost.

(d) The students to whom Aristotle was lecturing had already heard his lectures on ethics. He often assumes a familiarity with his *Ethics*, and hence refers to but does not elaborate points with which he had already dealt at length.

(e) All these difficulties exist even for those who can read the *Poetics* in the original Greek. But if we are dependent upon a translation there is a further difficulty; many Greek words have no English equivalent. The best that the translator can do is to use the nearest, but often misleading, English word ("action" for *praxeos*, "character" for *ēthos*, "imitation" for *mimesis*), or else to make a wordy explanatory paraphrase in an attempt to convey the meaning.

Nevertheless some knowledge of the *Poetics* is essential to an understanding of literary criticism. (1) It was Aristotle who started the whole business of the analysis of poetry and of the drama; all worthwhile criticism, from his own time to the present day, stems either directly or indirectly from him. Not only so; he still stands alone in his analysis of *the nature of the problems* presented by poetry; the questions which he asks are still as much as they ever were the fundamental ones which need answering. And even where he himself does not go all the way in finding an answer, always his suggestions point in the right direction. Later critics may have gone further than he has towards finding a solution, but it was he who first pointed the way. (2) All scholarly critics writing today assume a knowledge of Aristotle; they quote or refer to the *Poetics* expecting their readers to pick up the allusions; if we do not know to what they are referring we shall miss the point of what they are saying. (3) And unfortunately not only do scholarly critics quote Aristotle; the unscholarly *mis*-quote him. Either they have read and misunderstood him, or, more probably, they repeat at second-, third-, or a hundredth-hand certain statements as Aristotle's which are not in the *Poetics* at all. If one is not to be misled one must have read at least parts of the *Poetics* for oneself.

This chapter does not set out to be an exhaustive study of the *Poetics*; such a study would be far beyond the scope of this book, even were I, who am not a classical scholar, qualified to attempt it. What it does set out to do is to take certain key passages—those which you will most frequently find quoted or referred to in your critical reading, and which at the same time present difficulties or are liable to be misunderstood—to explain as simply as possible what Aristotle probably meant, and where there are differences of opinion as to his meaning to refer you to the most reliable authorities.

The translation which I am using is Bywater's *Aristotle on the Art of Poetry* (Oxford, Clarendon Press). You should have a copy by you while you read this chapter (it is a cheap paper-covered book). I shall quote the essential passages, but it is often necessary to read them in their context to see the full force of the argument. The commentaries which I am using are Humphry House's *Aristotle's Poetics* (Rupert Hart-Davies) and Butcher's *Aristotle's*

Theory of Poetry and Fine Art. Where they differ it is the former that I follow, and which I recommend if you want to follow up these notes with further reading. Not only is it the simplest introduction (it is based on lectures to students who knew no Greek), but where House's interpretation differs from those of Butcher and the other older commentators it is House's which most classical scholars today accept.

I am arranging my notes, apart from one or two cross-references, in the order in which the passages occur in the *Poetics*; the page references are to Bywater's translation.

(1) *Mimesis*, ch. 1, pp. 23–25; ch. 9, p. 43

"Epic poetry and Tragedy, as also Comedy, Dithyrambic poetry, *and most flute-playing and Lyre-playing*, are all, viewed as a whole, modes of imitation" (p. 23).

The Greek word here, and throughout the *Poetics*, translated "imitation" is *mimesis*; the words which I have italicized show clearly that the translation is misleading. For the idea which the word "imitation" suggests to us is of something which, while being in fact not the real thing, is intended to be such an exact copy of it as to deceive us into believing that it is: an imitation pearl is not a real one, but it is intended to look as if it were; the more deceptive the resemblance, the better the imitation. That this cannot here be Aristotle's meaning is evident; for what, other than themselves, can lute-playing or lyre-playing be mistaken? Those (and they are many) who accuse Aristotle of defining art as photographically accurate representation cannot have read this passage. And if you turn to ch. 9, p. 43, you will find the specific statement that poetry (the reference is to narrative and dramatic poetry) not only need not, but must not, be representational in the sense of being an accurate copy of the original: "From what we have said it will be seen that the poet's function is to describe, *not the thing that has happened, but a kind of thing which might happen*, i.e. what is possible as being probable or necessary." Which is to say that there is no existing original of which the poet sets out to make an exact copy.

In the English word "imitation" two ideas are present: (1) This is not the real thing, but (2) *it is intended to look as if it were.* In the Greek word *mimesis*, on the other hand, the stress is reversed: *This is not the real thing*, even though it bears some resemblance to an existing object or happening; *it is the work of an artist and not of nature*, and it must never pretend to be anything else. The poet's business is not to reproduce but to create.

Nevertheless, the poet's *mimesis* has a necessary relationship to "reality". Look again at page 43. After the passage which I have quoted Aristotle goes on to contrast history and (epic and dramatic) poetry: "the one describes the kind of thing which has been, the other a kind of thing which might be". He then continues:

> Hence poetry is something more philosophic and of graver import than history, *since its statements are of the nature of universals*, whereas those of history are singulars. By a universal statement I mean one as to what such and such a kind of man will probably or necessarily say or do—which is the aim of poetry . . .; by a singular statement one as to what, say, Alcibiades did or had done to him.

The "reality" which the poet "imitates" is human nature as such, the human passions as they are always and everywhere, but which in any given individual or situation in "real life" are obscured by innumerable accidental factors which confuse the issue. The poet's business is to create human beings as they would be if all these adventitious elements were excluded. The raw material of his *mimesis* is drawn from observation of, and insight into, human beings as they are, but his final creation is a picture of their fundamental passions and of the laws which govern them, purified of all extraneous matter. In narrative and dramatic poetry these passions are of course embodied in recognizable human beings, but once we accept that it is the passions themselves—"happiness and the reverse"—which the artist "imitates", then we see that *mimesis* covers even music; that too "imitates"—re-creates—these passions even though in a medium which can be mistaken for nothing but itself. All this is not to say that Aristotle would have gone all the way with modern non-representational art, but he was certainly no believer in photographic accuracy.

(2) *Tragedy and Comedy: Good and Bad Men*, ch. 2, pp. 26, 27; ch. 5, p. 33

"The objects the imitator represents are actions, with agents who are necessarily either good men or bad . . ." (p. 26). "This difference it is that distinguishes Tragedy and Comedy; the one would make its personages worse, and the other better, than the man of the present day" (pp. 26, 27). That is to say, *if we follow the translator*, tragedy is about people who are morally better, comedy about people who are morally worse, than our contemporaries, which is not true. With regard to comedy there is little difficulty; turn to ch. 5, p. 33:

> As for comedy it is (as has been observed) an imitation of people worse than the average: *worse, however, not as regards any and every sort of fault, but only as regards one particular kind, the ridiculous*. . . . The Ridiculous may be defined as a mistake or deformity not productive of pain or harm to others.

That is to say, the characters of comedy are not *morally* bad, they are merely *inferior* in that they are harmlessly foolish and laughable; the Greek word translated "bad" has no necessary moral implications. A greater difficulty arises with the use of "good" as a translation of the Greek *spoudaios*. The same word occurs in Aristotle's definition of tragedy (p. 35); here both Bywater and Butcher translate it by "serious", and Gilbert Murray (*Preface* to Bywater, p. 9) differentiates between tragedy and comedy as "high or low, serious or trivial". This seems to meet the case, but Humphry House rejects it and stands by "good". The sense in which tragedy can be said to be about "good" people will be clearer when we get to Aristotle's definition of the hero of tragedy.

(3) *Plot and Character*, ch. 6, pp. 36–37, 38

Aristotle has enumerated six elements in tragedy, of which character and plot are two. He then goes on:

> The most important of the six is the combination of the incidents in the story. Tragedy is essentially an imitation *not of persons but of action;* the end for which we live is a certain kind of activity, not a quality. Character gives us qualities, but it is in our actions—what we do—that we are happy

> or the reverse. In a play, accordingly, they do not act in order to portray character, they include the characters for the sake of the action [p. 37].

And (p. 38), "we maintain, therefore, that the first essential, *the life and soul, so to speak, of Tragedy, is Plot*".

The modern reader's first reaction to this is, almost invariably, violent disagreement. What would *Hamlet* be without the Prince of Denmark? It is his "character" which is the making of the play; what would the bare bones of the plot be without it? Yet even without further elucidation of Aristotle's meaning second thoughts may lead us to see that this is not quite the whole truth. Given the play as we have it, it is, of course, mainly in Hamlet's character that its greatness lies. But the play as we have it has a plot; eliminate the plot, or replace it by another, and where would Hamlet's character be? It is only in the setting not only of "a" plot, but of exactly the one which Shakespeare has chosen, that he comes into being at all. If nothing had happened to him, or if there had been a different set of happenings, not only would we not know what he had it in him to be, but he would not have become what, by the end of the play, he is.

But Aristotle goes very much further than this: he seems to suggest, not only that the plot is necessary if we are to have character, but that, given a good plot, a tragedy need not have "character" at all. But in fact Aristotle means nothing of the sort: the fault lies not in him but his translators; none of the three Greek words, *ēthos*, which is translated "character", *muthos*, "plot", or *praxeos*, "action", had the same meaning for the Greeks as have, for us, the English words by which Bywater has translated them. When we, in English, speak of a man's "character" we mean all that he is, *including how he behaves*, his habit, for instance, of actually losing his temper as well as an inherent tendency to be irritable to which he may never succumb; an unselfish person is not merely one who has it in him to consider others but one who in fact behaves unselfishly. The meaning of the Greek *ēthos* is far narrower; *it excludes behaviour* and is limited to a certain moral bent in a person's make-up, which may, *or may not*, express itself in action. But once it becomes active it ceases to be *ēthos* and becomes *praxeos*, the latter word thus including not only what we call action but the greater part of what we mean by character. And the word *muthos*, translated "plot", includes not only, as the English word suggests, the external happenings, the bare bones of the story with "character" left out, but every activity, mental, emotional, even verbal, by which *ēthos* becomes *praxeos*; in other words, what we call character is as much a part of *muthos* as is plot in our sense of the word. All that *muthos* excludes is moral tendencies—qualities—which have not expressed themselves in action. And quite clearly a play cannot be written round a man's mere potentialities; if Hamlet had only had a tendency towards melancholy and indecision which circumstances had never called into action and which hence had never influenced his behaviour there would have been no play. It is in this sense that Aristotle is using the words when he says that: "Tragedy is not an imitation of persons"—that is to say, of what people have it in them to be before their *ēthos* becomes *praxeos*—"but of action", "the end for which we live is a certain kind of activity and not a quality", and, "The first essential, the life and soul, so to speak of Tragedy, is Plot".

(4) *Plot: The Hero of Tragedy*, ch. 13, pp. 49–52

Here we come to what is commonly (and, in fact correctly) called Aristotle's definition of the Hero of Tragedy. The fact that he puts it under the heading of Plot, and in three out of his four examples describes plots and not characters, is explained by my last section: if *muthos* includes all that the hero does, then to define the *muthos* is also to define the hero.

Having restated (p. 49) the essential point of his definition of tragedy, that the Plot "must imitate actions arousing pity and fear", Aristotle goes on to enumerate three possible plots which are unsuitable for tragedy: (1) "A good man must not be seen passing from happiness to misery; or (2) a bad man from misery to happiness", nor (3) "an extremely bad man be seen falling from happiness into misery". (1) he dismisses, rather perfunctorily, as "odious"—that is to say, unbearably painful—and when we know, as we do when we come to his description of the ideal hero, that by "good" he here means completely good, coming to a bad end through absolutely no fault, or even mistake, of his own, we are inclined to agree; none of the great tragedies fall into this category. In the case of (2) the question of whether it was a tragic plot would not today arise: we confine the word tragedy to plays ending in death or disaster. But to the Greeks there were only two kinds of drama, serious (tragedy) and ridiculous (comedy); a serious play—one dealing with a situation productive of pity and fear—was a tragedy even if, as it is in the *Iphigenia in Tauris*, the final disaster is averted. But Aristotle's (2) has nothing in common with this, and he, as would we, dismisses it as "the most untragic that can be". We now come to (3), "an extremely bad man falling from happiness to misery; . . . *it will not move us either to pity or fear; pity is occasioned by undeserved misfortune, and fear by that of one like ourselves*". Here we have a test case in Shakespeare's *Richard III*, and we have only to compare its impact upon us with that of any great tragedy to recognize how right Aristotle is: it arouses nothing of the authentic tragic emotion. And this for exactly the reasons which Aristotle gives: however fascinated we may have been by the ruthless evil of Richard's character, and perhaps awed by his fall, our reaction to his end (and the reaction which Shakespeare most certainly intended) is not pity but relief that England is rid of such a tyrant. And as to fear, we have not identified ourselves with such heartless cruelty and hence we feel no fear that a like fate will befall us. The play is the perfect justification of Aristotle. (And this whatever Butcher may say to the contrary.)

Having thus eliminated three possible, but faulty, plots, Aristotle goes on (p. 50) to define the right one: "There remains, then, the intermediate kind of personage, *a man not pre-eminently virtuous and just*, whose misfortune, however, is brought upon him *not by vice or depravity but by some error of judgement*, of the number of those in the enjoyment of great reputation and prosperity." That is to say, on the one hand, the hero is not a passive victim of external circumstance; *he has himself contributed to his own downfall;*

on the other hand, his contribution has been *a mere mistake*, and in all other respects he is a good man—better, in fact, than the average—one with whom we can both sympathize and identify ourselves and whom we pity because his misfortune is out of all proportion to his initial error. "Of the number of those in the enjoyment of great reputation and prosperity": the greater the height from which he falls the more his fall moves us. This definition satisfies us—it covers the hero of every great tragedy—except for the one phrase, "error of *judgement*". Surely something more than faulty judgement was involved in the downfall of Hamlet, of Othello, of Lear, or of Phèdre, or of any of the heroes of Greek tragedy other than Oedipus? Were not their errors moral as well as intellectual?

How Aristotle himself would have answered this question depends upon the meaning he attached to the word translated "error of judgement", *hamartia*, and this is one of the most controversial points in the interpretation of the *Poetics*. Can, or cannot, *hamartia* be stretched to cover a moral error? Butcher, and Gilbert Murray in his preface (p. 11) to Bywater's translation, say that it can. Both acknowledge that its primary meaning was a mistake as to a matter of fact, but both add a secondary meaning, an error of *moral* judgement, a sin, the mistake of an otherwise good man who, on one occasion, chooses evil instead of good. This satisfies us: Lear not only made the intellectual error of believing Goneril's and Regan's flattery, but the moral one of giving way to his ungovernable rage; Macbeth's initial "mistake" in listening to the witches lay not only in believing what they said but in toying with what he knew was the temptation to commit murder. And so on with the rest. Butcher goes further in adding a third meaning, a defect of character, the "fatal flaw" from which all the ensuing errors spring. But for this (whether tragic heroes tend to have "fatal flaws" or not) there seems to be no other authority; it is an example of Butcher's habit of stretching Aristotle's meaning to fit his own pre-conceptions; we can dismiss it. But Humphry House rejects even Butcher's and Gilbert Murray's second meaning; he limits the meaning of the word solely to *a mistake as to the facts*; the hero, though better than the average man, has, it is true, moral faults, but the *hamartia* which brings about his downfall is not these faults but one specific mistake as to the facts of the situation. Oedipus could not know that the old man he killed was his father or the woman he married was his mother, but it was these mistakes, and not a moral fault, which caused his tragedy.

This does not mean, however, that Aristotle made no allowance for those moral faults or weaknesses which may have led the hero to make his one mistake—even for a "fatal flaw", although nothing which he says suggests that he was thinking in such terms. But these faults of "character" (in our sense of the word) are indicated, not by the word *hamartia*, but by "not pre-eminently virtuous and just". He is distinguishing between two necessary elements in the tragic plot: (1) the hero's character; he must be a predominantly good, but faulty, man, not a paragon of virtue; one without vices but with human weaknesses; and (2) the actual incident in the plot which precipitates his downfall; it is this which must be a "mistake". And these two elements are, in fact, present in almost all the great tragedies (Oedipus is a rare exception); the hero has faults which contribute to his "mistake", but the tragic irony consists in the fact that these faults in themselves would not have brought his misfortune upon him had it not been for his one avoidable "error of judgement". Lear had an ungovernable temper, but from the point of view of plot it was not his temper in itself (for had it been directed against Goneril and Regan all would have been well), but his mistaken judgement of the characters of his three daughters which set in motion the chain of cause and effect which is the "action" of the play. So of Othello: he misjudged Iago's "honesty"; had he not made this one error of judgement his passions would never have been aroused. And this even of Hamlet, though here the case is far more complex: had he not made the one factual mistake of doubting the Ghost's veracity, and hence of postponing bringing Claudius to justice before it was too late, there would have been no plot.

So much for *hamartia*. We now return to the question: how good should the hero of tragedy be? Certainly good enough to engage our sympathies and pity. But Aristotle undoubtedly intended more than this: the hero, whatever his weaknesses, must be above ourselves, someone we can look up to. The grandeur of tragedy—its power to produce the *catharsis* of pity and fear—lies just in this: that a man so good should yet "make a mistake". His faults must be only such as to make us feel that he is a human being like ourselves. Aristotle would almost certainly have ruled out Macbeth—such a character would have been contrary to his whole conception of tragedy. He would not have allowed for the possibility of such a murderer engaging our sympathies. And of course a mere murderer, such as Richard III, cannot; what Shakespeare has done in *Macbeth* is to create a man who when the play opens, before he has made his "error of judgement", *is* a "good" man—that is to say, a man of nobility and honour, with a conscience, a desire for goodness (look at Lady Macbeth's summing-up of his character after she has read his letter), himself horrified at his own evil imaginings, as Richard III could not conceivably have been—and to show this man, potentially so much better than the average, yet making the two fatal mistakes of, first, toying with the witches' temptation, and then, against his own better judgement, allowing himself to be persuaded by his wife. But to Greek tragedy, which was all that Aristotle knew, such a hero would have been entirely alien. We can be wise after the event and see that, given sufficient initial nobility, even a man who later in the play becomes a murderer can move us to pity and fear. But Aristotle, who lived approximately two thousand years before Shakespeare, cannot be blamed for not foreseeing the possibility.

Unity, chs. 7 and 8; pp. 39–43

Here we come to the supreme "literary superstition" (as Butcher calls it) with regard to Aristotle's *Poetics*: the common belief that it is the source of the neo-classical rule of "The Three Unities". *To Aristotle there was one unity and one only, Unity of Action* (or, a better translation, of Plot). Of the so-called Unities of Time and Place *he says nothing*; for him they are no part of the conception of unity at all. He never once, in the whole of the *Poetics*, uses the word "unity" in any connection but that of Plot. The doctrine of the "Unities of Time and Place" was the invention of late sixteenth-century neo-classicism. (How it came to be invented will come later.)

So to the only Unity which Aristotle recognizes: Plot. Turn first to page 40:

> . . . a tragedy is an imitation of an action *that is complete in itself, as a whole* of some magnitude. Now a whole is that which has *beginning, middle and end*. A beginning is that which is not necessarily after anything else, and which has naturally something after it; and end is that which is naturally after something else, either as its necessary or usual consequent, and with nothing after it; and a middle, that which is by nature after one thing, and has also something after it.

This is not a description of real life: in "life" there are no such things as beginnings or ends, as Aristotle defines them: everything is a middle. We are what we are—and hence do what we do—because our parents were what they were and did what they did, including marrying each other and not someone else. So, in their turn, of them and their parents, and so on and so on back to Adam—or to the amoeba. And after our deaths the chains of cause and effect which we have set in motion will go on to the end of time. One thing always both follows from, and leads to, another, unendingly. But this is not how plays are made. The business of the writer of tragedy is to create unity, wholeness—a beginning, a middle and an end—where in life it does not exist. And he does this by choosing as his beginning some one single situation of which, although in fact it must have had causes, the causes play no part in the chain of cause and effect which is the "action" of the play. The situation is "given"; we do not need to know what brought it about in order to explain its consequences. King Lear had two bad daughters and one good one; it is from that, and not from whatever factors in their heredity and upbringing made them what they were, that the action springs. The middle is the series of happenings which arise out of this situation, and from nothing else. The end is the point at which the consequences of the initial situation have worked themselves out to their conclusion and at which every question which the play has made us ask has been answered; what in real life would have followed does not concern us. At the end of *Hamlet* we do not ask how Fortinbras governed Denmark; the action has been concerned solely with Hamlet himself, Claudius and Gertrude, and with Polonius and Ophelia in so far as they were involved in it. All our questions have been about them and they are answered.

Now turn to ch. 8, p. 41. "The Unity of Plot does not consist, as some suppose, in its having one man as its subject. An infinity of things befall that one man, some of which it is impossible to reduce to unity, and in like manner there are many actions of one man which cannot be made to form one action." Taking "one action" to mean, as Aristotle intends it to, the chain of cause and effect which leads from the beginning, through the middle, to the end, the meaning of this passage is, I think, quite clear. Aristotle then goes on to illustrate his point by contrasting the (legendary) life of Odysseus with the "action" of the *Odyssey*, showing what Homer was obliged to omit in order to achieve unity as he has defined it. Finally (p. 42), comes the summing up: ". . . in poetry the story, as an imitation of action, must represent one action, *with its several incidents so closely connected that the transposal or withdrawal of any one of them will disjoin or dislocate the whole.*" You will see that this is only another way of expressing the "therefore . . . therefore" which we have already defined as constituting the perfect plot in a novel.

The Unities of Time and Place

These, as we have seen, have nothing whatsoever to do with Aristotle, but as they are so frequently attributed to him it is as well that you should know how they did originate and become the rule of neo-classical drama.

The duration of the action of a Greek play was, in fact, generally, though far from always, limited to a period of twenty-four hours, and, again only generally, was confined to one place. Aristotle says (ch. 5, p. 34): "Tragedy endeavours to keep as far as possible within a single circuit of the sun, or something near that." Of place he says nothing. (His remark (p. 82) that in Tragedy it is not possible, as it is in Epic, to include a number of simultaneous incidents—that is, incidents happening simultaneously in different places—is a self-evident truth, as applicable to Shakespearean, or modern, drama as to Greek.) But as to what he says of time there are two things to note:

(1) He is stating *a fact as to what Greek drama did*; he is not, as he does with Plot, laying down a rule as to what all drama ought to do.

(2) *Even this fact he in no way relates to Unity;* he merely mentions it in passing in a chapter on a totally different topic, the differences between Tragedy and Epic.

The fact is that the usual limitation of the action of a Greek play to a duration of twenty-four hours and to one place had nothing to do with aesthetic theory; it was simply a practical solution of a practical problem: the presence of the Chorus. The Chorus (a) were characters in the play; and (b) could never leave the stage, for it was their function to chant Choric Odes between the acts. With regard to time, it is perfectly clear that verisimilitude would be strained to breaking point were a group of characters to remain upon the scene, visible to the audience, for what was supposed to be a matter of months or years. "One circuit of the sun" we can accept, for granted that we are sufficiently absorbed in the action of the play, we do not stop to notice that the action must have occupied a few more hours than the two or three which is all that the play has lasted. And even a duration of some weeks can, in exceptional circumstances, be accepted: in *The Suppliants* of Euripides Theseus marches forty miles, fights a battle, and returns victorious between the end of one act and the beginning of the next. Impossible—but it does not matter, for the audience's attention has been so fully occupied by what is happening on the stage—the words of the Chorus—

that they have none to spare to count the miles of the march or the hours of the battle. It is an extreme example of what Granville-Barker, in writing of Shakespeare, calls "elastic time"—time which the dramatist makes us feel has passed quickly, although when we stop to think we know must have been of considerable duration. But even so there is a limit beyond which this "willing suspension of belief" cannot be strained, and, given the presence of the Chorus, *The Suppliants* probably reaches it.

And the presence of the Chorus accounts, too, for the usual limitation of the action to one place: obviously if a group of citizens of Thebes are continuously present on the stage the scene cannot suddenly become Corinth, or how would the Thebans have got there? The only possibility of change of scene is that the Chorus themselves, in the course of their Choric Ode between two acts, should be supposed to be making the journey from one city to the other. And this does happen in the *Eumenides*; the Chorus are the Furies and in the interval between two acts they pursue Orestes from Delphi to Athens; when the next act opens we accept the fact that the scene is now Athens and no longer Delphi. Thus (a) there was no rule that the action should be confined to one place, and (b) even when it was so confined it was of practical necessity and had no connection with unity.

The Unities of Time and Place, far from being Aristotelean, were first formulated by a neo-classical writer, Castelvetro, as late as 1570. As you already know, among the marks of neo-classicism (from the Renaissance onwards) were a blind and slavish imitation of the forms of classical art, and the practice of reducing to rule what the Greeks had done by instinct or necessity. The neo-classicist scholars made the discovery that the action of most Greek plays was confined to a period of twenty-four hours and to one place. (They do not seem to have noticed the exceptions.) If the Greeks did it it must be the right thing to do; the only question was, why? Not realizing the true reason—the presence of the Chorus—they had to invent one of their own: to have no break in time or change of place made for unity. And to this they added another reason: verisimilitude. Assuming the fallacy that a play, to be credible, must be mistaken for reality they argued that it was impossible while sitting in the theatre to believe that more hours had passed than the play had taken to perform (they jibbed even at Aristotle's "one circuit of the sun"), or that a stage that in one act the audience had actually believed to be Thebes could in the next be accepted as Corinth. This, of course shows a complete misunderstanding not only of the nature of dramatic illusion but of Aristotle's own principle of *mimesis*. Yet it was blindly and unthinkingly accepted as a self-evident truth by the majority of neo-classical critics (Dryden was a shining exception) until Samuel Johnson, by sheer humorous common sense, exploded it in his *Preface to Shakespeare*.

Conclusion

These, together with *catharsis*, with which I have dealt in a previous chapter, are the passages in the *Poetics* which you are most likely to find quoted (or misquoted), or else assumed as part of the educated reader's stock of knowledge. There is much else in the *Poetics* which will repay study, but these points are the essentials.

SUGGESTIONS FOR FURTHER READING

On Poetry

P. B. Shelley, *A Defence of Poetry*.
A unique expression of the romantic philosophy of poetry.

W. Wordsworth, "Preface" to the second edition of *Lyrical Ballads*, in *The Poetical Works of William Wordsworth*, O.U.P.
Wordsworth's arrangement of his material makes this difficult reading. It is a help to start in the middle with the definition of the poet (the paragraph beginning, "Taking up the subject then upon general grounds . . .") and then go back to the beginning.

S. T. Coleridge, *Biographia Literaria*.
A beginner is recommended to use the selections in the Nonsuch Press's *Coleridge*, in which Coleridge's confusing digressions are omitted.

John Keats, *Letters of John Keats*, ed. Sidney Colvin, Macmillan.
Besides much that is personal the letters contain profound reflections on the nature of poetry and of the imagination.

These are fundamental texts in which the romantic poets speak for themselves. They may be supplemented with:

W. Hazlitt, "Of Poetry in General" in *Hazlitt's Selected Essays*, Nonsuch Press.

For eighteenth-century criticism at its greatest:

Samuel Johnson, *Lives of the Poets*, especially "Milton", "Dryden", and "Pope".

And for the Victorian period:

Matthew Arnold, *Essays in Criticism, Second Series*, Macmillan.

Of more recent studies the following are recommended:

Lascelles Abercrombie, *The Theory of Poetry*. Martin Secker.
Especially the chapter "Inspiration and Form".

T. R. Henn, *The Apple and the Spectroscope*, Methuen.
A most perceptive introduction to poetry, intended for students of science and mathematics, but helpful to the literary student.

Cecil Day Lewis, *Poetry for You*, Basil Blackwell.
An introduction written for children, but it contains much, especially the chapters "How a Poem is Made" and "When is a Poem not a Poem?", which will help more mature readers if they are not repelled by the sometimes childish presentation.

Cecil Day Lewis, *The Poetic Image*, Jonathan Cape.
Indispensable for advanced readers.

I. A. Richards, *Practical Criticism*, Routledge & Kegan Paul.

Of great value if read with the reservations I have suggested in Chapter 1.

Helen Gardner, *The Business of Criticism*, Clarendon Press.

The first section, *The Profession of a Critic*, states the case for scholarly research and against "Practical Criticism".

Ed. John Wain, *Interpretations*, Routledge & Kegan Paul.

Examples of "Practical Criticism" as it is practised today, showing the method both at its best and at its not so good.

F. R. Leavis, *Revaluation*, Chatto & Windus.

In spite of the perversity of some of the author's judgements this book should be read both for the merits of certain of the essays and as a landmark in the history of contemporary taste.

J. Livingstone Lowes, *The Road to Xanadu*, Constable.

For an appraisal of this book see p. 25.

H. J. C. Grierson, *Rhetoric and English Composition*, Oliver & Boyd, Edinburgh.

A course of lectures intended as a guide to the writing of both prose and poetry, but as valuable to readers as to writers. A comprehensive survey of the different styles used by poets and prose writers, and of how they achieve their effects.

Drama

Aristotle, *On the Art of Poetry*, translated by Ingram Bywater, Clarendon Press.

Humphry House, *Aristotle's Poetics*, Rupert Hart-Davies.

S. H. Butcher, *Aristotle's Theory of Poetry and Fine Art*, Paperback Edition, Dover Publications, New York.

This was the standard book on the *Poetics* until it was superseded by Humphry House, and it is still of value to those who wish to pursue the subject.

John Dryden, "An Essay of Dramatic Poesy" in *Dramatic Essays*, Everyman's Library.

One of the classics of English dramatic criticism.

Samuel Johnson, *Preface to Shakespeare* in *Johnson on Shakespeare*, O.U.P.

Another critical classic whose sanity provides an essential corrective to the transcendentalism of romantic Shakespearean criticism.

S. T. Coleridge, Selections from his Shakespearean criticism in the Nonsuch Press's *Coleridge*.

A. C. Bradley, *Shakespearean Tragedy*, Macmillan.

Although many of Bradley's judgements have been rejected by later critics this still remains a great work of interpretation.

Harley Granville-Barker, *Prefaces to Shakespeare*, First and Second Series. Sidgwick & Jackson.

The books (the first published in 1927) which brought Shakespearean criticism back from the study to the stage.

U. ELLIS-FERMOR, *The Frontiers of Drama*, Methuen.
Stimulating studies of various aspects of drama.

GEORGE MEREDITH, *Essay on Comedy*, Constable.
To be read with caution; one cannot accept all Meredith's judgements.

BONAMY DOBRÉE, *Restoration Comedy*, O.U.P.
An excellent study not only of the individual comic dramatists of the period but also of the origins and nature of the Comedy of Manners.

THE CLASSICAL AND THE ROMANTIC

SIR MAURICE BOWRA, *The Greek Experience*, Weidenfeld & Nicolson.
A beautifully illustrated book on the Greeks, their civilization and their art, as scholarly as it is attractive.

SIR MAURICE BOWRA, *The Romantic Imagination*, O.U.P.
Chapter 1 is indispensable as an introduction to the romantic conception of the imagination. It is followed by studies of the individual English romantic poets.

COLERIDGE, WORDSWORTH, SHELLEY, KEATS — The works already listed under "Poetry".

T. E. HULME, The essay "Classical and Romantic" in *Speculations*, Routledge Paperback.
Whatever one may think of Hulme's over-statement of the case against romanticism, this essay, published in 1924, is a historical document of the first importance for its influence on the twentieth-century swing of taste from the romantic to the classical.

T. S. ELIOT, *Selected Essays*, Faber & Faber.
The essay "Tradition and the Individual Talent" (1917) stands with Hulme's essay as a manifesto of the new classicism, but it is far the more balanced and profound of the two.

T. S. ELIOT, *The Use of Poetry and the Use of Criticism*, Faber & Faber.
An invaluable statement of the classical conception of poetry, but it stresses only the faults of romanticism.

F. L. LUCAS, *The Decline and Fall of the Romantic Ideal*, Cambridge University Press.
A perceptive study of the merits and defects of both classicism and romanticism. The author's bias is towards the classical.

THE NOVEL

E. M. FORSTER, *Aspects of the Novel*, Edward Arnold.
Indispensable, even though one may not agree with all the author's judgements.

PERCY LUBBOCK, *The Craft of Fiction*, Jonathan Cape.
Especially notable for the author's exposition of the principle of "The Point of View".

WALTER ALLEN, *The English Novel*, Penguin Books.
An excellent short history of the English novel; the critical evaluations of the great novelists could hardly be bettered. Strongly recommended.

V. S. PRITCHETT, *The Living Novel*, Chatto & Windus.
Short studies of a variety of novelists, English, French and Russian. Excellent within its limits.

LORD DAVID CECIL, *Early Victorian Novelists*, Constable.
Perceptive studies of the great Early Victorians, from which can be deduced standards of judgement applicable to other novelists.

F. R. LEAVIS, *The Great Tradition*, Chatto & Windus.
Whether or not one agrees with the author's pre-suppositions this is an important book on account of its influence on contemporary taste.

HENRY FIELDING, Introductory chapters to the eighteen books of *Tom Jones*.
Fielding was the first novelist to treat novel-writing as an art and many of his dicta in these chapters go to the root of the matter.

HENRY JAMES, "Prefaces" to the New York edition of his novels, collected in *The Art of the Novel*, Scribner.
Another novelist writing on his own art.

INDEX